Veganism of Color

JULIA FELIZ BRUECK

A Vegans-of-Color Community Project

Sanctuary Publishers

DEDICATION

To Wolfram, Danae, Michelle, Dani, Starr, LoriKim, and everyone that has taken a chance on me and my never-ending passion and projects.

To all of you working towards a world that is *consistently anti-oppression* so that, one day, we may *all* be free.

CONTENTS

ACKNOWLEDGMENTS

Thank you to each and every Vegan of Color that added their voice to this community-led project. Your words are invaluable in helping to building bridges towards achieving justice for all.

An immense thank you to graphic designer Danae Silva Montiel – your artistic talents never cease to amaze and fill me with wonder.

Last but not least, thank you to the organization Deutscher Jugendschutz-Verband for your kind support, which helped bring this project to life.

I'm truly grateful for each and every one of you – this project would not exist without you.

To the reader, thank you for being open to our perspectives. We hope our words will be the start of conversations and inspire the continual changes needed for us all to find liberation from all forms of oppression.

A Note to White Vegans

Race does matter in conversations related to nonhuman animal rights. There is racism in the vegan and animal rights movement, and there is racism in the conceptualization of animals. So, it's non-negotiable that we must address this issue.

−Carol J. Adams, 2018

While you are welcome to read and learn from Vegans of Color, this book is specifically a conversation between Vegans of Color and People of Color. Unless you have started doing the work to acknowledge and address your role in the systemic oppression of People of Color and other marginalized groups, this book will most likely not make sense to you in your current world view.

In addition, you will do more damage than good when attempting to raise the voices of nonhuman animals within communities about which you know little or nothing. Black vegan scholar and critical race theorist Dr. A. Breeze Harper explained that, "Unfortunately, low racial literacy and the lack of more inclusive frameworks from vegan organizations and individuals has negatively affected how racial minorities such as Black people in the U.S.A. engage with animal advocacy. This, in turn, impacts everyone's potential to alleviate the suffering of nonhuman animals."

Thus, you must stay in your lane, focus on your own communities, and begin doing the work to understand the world beyond your sole experiences. Doing the work includes self-reflection about the history of nonhuman oppression as it relates to racism and white settlers' role in perpetuating both human and nonhuman animal abuses, as well as recognizing your privileges over other marginalized groups and acknowledging how you may add to the unfortunate fact that mainstream veganism is oppressive in itself.

If you have not done so, please read the books *Veganism in an Oppressive World*, edited by Julia Feliz Brueck and *Food Justice: A Primer*, edited by Saryta Rodríguez. Please also take the time to read through the *Vegan Bill of Consistent Anti-Oppression,* which is hosted on the site ConsistentAntiOppression.com.

Resources like these will help you become aware of interconnections between social justice movements and how to help veganism become a movement that does not add to the oppression of other marginalized groups.

PREFACE

Mainstream white veganism is white supremacy. You've known that, and we, Vegans of Color, agree. It doesn't represent us– and never will.

Mainstream white veganism is rooted in saviorism through single-issue advocacy in which whiteness, yet again, places a group of marginalized beings (nonhumans) above People of Color and other oppressed groups. In this way, this type of white-centered advocacy places whiteness at the top while employing, without consent, nonhumans as a tool to further oppress us.

We Vegans of Color reject this; we reject a veganism (and any social justice movement) that allows any form of oppression to continue in our name. Racism, xenophobia, classism, homophobia, transphobia, ableism, ageism, anti-Semitism, anti-blackness, islamophobia, casteism, health shaming, body shaming, and any other "ism" does not have a place in any movement working towards justice. Our fight also includes taking an active stance against *speciesism* –a form of supremacy with white supremacy at its roots, in which we People of Color are used as tools of oppression against other living beings, perpetuating our own oppression in a never-ending cycle.

We know both "veganism" and "speciesism" are white words made up by some of the most privileged humans on the planet. While our communities were fighting against segregation, blatant discrimination, and towards gaining basic rights, white people had the privilege to name a form of oppression and living that was more common to Communities of Color before they entered our countries and pillaged our ways of life to the ground– after all, they did introduce the "food" animals that make up the majority of our meals in places like the U.S. and later, jumpstart the intense livestock-farming systems that exacerbated the destruction of our planet's health. Regardless, neither of these concepts belong to whiteness, and we must attempt to reclaim them as we work towards making connections towards our own liberation.

When speaking about veganism, a term that describes actively rejecting the exploitation of nonhuman animals, we will be speaking about *veganism of color*, which extends beyond single-issue activism and embraces a veganism that is consistent in anti-oppression; one that is mindful about interconnecting oppressions; one that applies to us, the world's majority; and one that ensures we are aware of and working against specific forms of speciesism, including *racialized speciesism* and *casteist speciesism*, forced upon us in an effort to render us willing participants in our own oppression.

White supremacy, through colonialism, successfully implemented hierarchies not just between the "races" they classified us into (some which it forcibly created) but between humans and non-human animal species as well. This specific hierarchy between species made it possible to create a divide between our own communities and the natural world. The knee-jerk reaction that we experience when we are called any number of nonhumans as an insult is what we have internalized as *racialized speciesism*. It is a subconscious need to separate ourselves from those who are considered the lowest on the supremacist ladder because they are the farthest removed from whiteness. By doing this, we reinforce our place in the hierarchy as "less than" and actively keep ourselves caught under white supremacy's rule.

In an excerpt from the chapter "Making Connections in the Name of Food" published in the book *Food Justice: A Primer* (2018) I explained that,

Nonhumans have been traditionally "otherized," meaning they have been denigrated, denied personhood, and marginalized due to their obvious

3

differences to humans, in order to justify them as "less than." In turn, nonhumans have been used to marginalize and justify the oppression of Black and Brown humans, forced to live in a system that protects whiteness as the "top" and "right" way to be. In this system, Black and Brown humans subconsciously learned and accepted to uphold their own otherization by also viewing and treating nonhumans as "less than" under what can be described as racialized speciesism (in my view, an aspect of speciesism experienced by people of color). This has culminated in a supremacist hierarchical relationship between all animals, human and nonhuman alike, which continues to ensure the survival of the oppressor/oppressed relationship that permeates myriad aspects of social justice, including food justice.

How has this worked? Animalization, even though we are all biological animals, is a tactic often employed to otherize marginalized groups. Donald Trump's latest comments on immigrants is an example of this, and we can see more examples of this tactic and how we reinforce it in the way we communicate daily. Consider something as basic as language and how terms that are even used today work to denigrate people of color, the disabled, and the poor, to name a few. How many commonly used words and phrases that we currently use originate from descriptions associated with nonhumans in a derogatory light (i.e. beast, pig, bitch, vulture, rat, savage, etc....)? How do those words continue to uphold the divide between humans (biologically animals) and nonhuman animals, the latter of whom are not even recognized as individual communities with their own languages, habitats, means of survival, and so forth? Subconsciously, we have played into our own version of supremacy and unwillingly and unquestioningly uphold it through the way we speak. Simply put, the language that we use reinforces the "less than" perception that humans have accepted of nonhumans without question. The same language is then continually employed to justify the perception that humans that do not fit a certain type are also "less than."

Importantly, you will find that other oppressive systems, like *casteism*, also depend on nonhumans as a tool of oppression over marginalized castes— not only through language but also through food and the bodies of other animals themselves.

In essence, the words printed on the following pages will raise the voices of Vegans of Color to bring our own communities an understanding of what we propose: the need to decenter whiteness from a movement rooted in rejecting our own hand in supremacy over all living beings because nonhuman liberation is tied to our own and because ethics are not owned by whiteness or by those from the most privileged castes. For far too long, the conversations on animal rights and human supremacy have focused on a single, privileged point of view. Therefore, with each chapter of this book, we attempt to take back something that also belongs to us, beyond what the most privileged have led our communities to believe.

[handwritten margin note: Feliz Brueck's arg.]

The stories you will read are those based on individual journeys through intersecting identities and experiences written by everyday People of Color from all different walks of life across the globe attempting to raise our voices above whiteness (and casteism) so that you may learn how our liberation is tied to each other's and the need to ensure that our efforts towards justice extend beyond ourselves.

Julia Feliz Brueck

1 INTRODUCTION

Decentering Whiteness as the Narrative
By Dr. Linda Alvarez

Generally, veganism has been understood as the practice of abstaining from the use of animal products. While distinctions have been made between dietary vegans, "vegan foodies," ethical vegans, environmental vegans and, recently, pro-intersectional vegans, the underlying thread is the avoidance of the exploitation of animals— albeit to varying degrees.

Reference to the vegan "movement" is a bit more specific, since movements carry social, political, and economic connotations. Historically, this movement has been focused on challenging the engrained idea that nonhuman animals are commodities that can and should be used to meet human needs. Generally, the mainstream vegan movement has focused on animal welfare. However, there are more critical spaces within the vegan movement that advocate for the total liberation of animals.

As with other social movements, as different groups have participated in the vegan movement, different aspects of the movement itself have been challenged. One aspect of the mainstream vegan movement that has received much pushback, as more and more People of Color (PoC) have become vegan, is the notion that veganism is a "white thing" or that "only white people are vegan." This pushback stems from the recognition that a dominant, white narrative, which remains an extremely problematic aspect of this movement, has crafted the vegan movement, especially in the United States. Because mainstream factions of this movement, which also happen to be the most heavily-funded parts of the movement, have been so greatly influenced by white vegan perspectives and have not been inclusive of narratives of color, whiteness, along with elite and privileged ideas, has been centered in the movement. Thus, it has been the case that when PoC attempt to engage the vegan movement, they are met with a myriad of problematic issues.

For example, in the vegan movement, PoC have had to confront the use of images of violence against PoC humans shown alongside images of animals being subject to seemingly similar types of violence in order to create a "mental link" between human and nonhuman suffering. The goal being that this "link" will push people toward veganism. Yet, there are two important questions here. First, why do the attempts at forging this "mental link", this emotional connection, always involve People of Color and nonhuman animals in contexts of violence? One of the most problematic images used in this type of "vegan propaganda" is the image of Black person (we are never informed on the context, or at the very least who this person is; we only see this person's objectification) that has been lynched, juxtaposed with a picture of a pig hanging from a back leg, presumably dead. Explanations for the use of this image have attempted to connect the slavery of humans and nonhuman animals and the violence inherent in these systems. Ultimately, the goal of the message is that if we, as humans, reject the slavery of humans, then we also should reject the "slavery" of animals. A proper understanding of why this is problematic is beyond the scope of this piece, but at its most basic level, we should understand that the systematic enslavement of African people and the pain attached to that violence is not, nor should ever be used as, propaganda. Therein lies one of the fundamental issues – that violence against People of Color has been used as propaganda in the mainstream vegan "movement." This tells us a lot about the dynamics of power that have shaped the dissemination of information within this "movement."

The second question here is a bit more abstract – we should all wonder why we need to understand the violence, and or suffering, toward animals through the lens of human experience. Many have pondered this question. The simplest answer is because it's relatable. If we can relate to the pain, we can sympathize, and perhaps be motivated to act. Statements like, "A mother cow cries when her calf is taken away, how would you like it if someone took your child away?" remain within this framework of relatability. The example above also attempts to utilize relatability to make a point. No doubt, these relational approaches will incite an emotional response in some people. However, if our activism for nonhuman living beings has to relate to us first, then it remains limited, and prioritizes, our scope of relatability rather than the needs of the other. If this concept remains unclear, consider the reactions most people, many vegans included, will have, when considering protecting the lives of insects. The villainized cockroach, or the spider, or worms, very rarely fall into our framework of relatability and therefore, protection.

Returning to the matter of issues faced by PoC within the movement, we also find the common rhetoric calling for the criminalization of nonwhite people who work in spaces where animals are subjected to extreme violence and death, such as slaughterhouses. Similarly, often within vegan spaces, the exploitable labor of PoC is normalized. I recall being on a panel at a VegFest event in Los Angeles where a member of the audience asked the panel what an ideal vegan world would look like. The white male vegan on the panel responded that factory farms would be shut down (the crowd cheered), and the world would be full of plant-based farms from which we would all nourish ourselves. I questioned (out loud) who would be doing the labor in this "ideal" world? Who are the farm workers here? Before he answered, I posited the need to consider in *whose* version of an "ideal" vegan world does an exploited PoC labor class still exist?

Not in mine.

PoC communities are also targeted with the rhetoric that going vegan is "easy and affordable" for everyone. Since white people have shaped the mainstream vegan movement, it lacks the cultural competence that would be relevant and important for PoC not only within social, political, and economic narratives but also in the practical aspects of veganism. Take for example the optics of "PoC vegan food" as displayed through the white experience: A hard, boat-shaped "taco" shell stuffed with tofu, lettuce, tomatoes and vegan "cheese" is presented as a delicious "Mexican" dish that can draw people of Latin American descent into veganism. Two things here: First, not all people of Latin American descent are Mexican. Second, hard-shell "tacos" are not tacos; they're blasphemy.

The lack of understanding of different cultures is alienating and often off-putting to Communities of Color. It is in this context that the perspective that veganism is a "white thing" is, unfortunately, advanced.

Challenging the Dominant Narrative

White dominance in the vegan movement is a real thing, but to say that veganism is only for white people is erroneous. When we, as People of Color, advance this narrative, we serve to invisiblize the work that non-white people have done for veganism and disappear the communities of color that have been practicing veganism before it was coined as a term. Because of this, I would like to challenge once and for all the idea that veganism is a "white thing" and propose a different framework of understanding.

To be clear, I am not positing that a "white" and privileged narrative has *not* dominated the vegan movement, and that such narrative should not be addressed and corrected. However, as People of Color, if we engage the vegan movement while taking as a point of departure that the vegan movement is inherently white, then we have already allowed our experience with veganism to be subsumed by the white dominant discourse of the mainstream movement. The fact of the matter is that the vegan movement does not belong to any one group. If we are to allocate "ownership" to any group, logic would dictate that it should be a group of people who advocate for the total liberation of nonhuman animals independent of the color or culture of the people in said group. Yet, the white narrative has dominated the movement for so long that as PoC challenge this discourse, one of the questions we have to ask ourselves is why non-white vegans and their contributions to veganism have historically been invisiblized in the movement, and whether or not our focus on whiteness has served to maintain this invisibility. That is, if we as PoC continue to focus on white people, we continue to center whiteness. Alternatively, we can understand the dynamics of power that have historically shaped the vegan movement and then work to create counter narratives.

The Overfocus on Whiteness: At What Cost?

As People of Color, we understand that a white-upper-class narrative dominates the world. We live in a world of social constructs, where one of the most oppressive of those constructs is racial hierarchy, which then operates in conjunction with class to create violent conditions for non-white and poor people around the world. Because we are raised and socialized within this paradigm, we often view the world through this dominant lens, internalizing and unfortunately, some-times even reproducing this oppressive perspective.

I challenge you to consider what we are really saying when we say veganism is a "white thing"? First, we are positioning ourselves outside of the vegan movement and are relinquishing our agency within this space. In doing so, we have to ask ourselves: If veganism is the notion that animals should be liberated and not ex-ploited, oppressed, violently abused, and indiscrimina-tely killed by humans, are only white people capable of embracing this philosophy? Are only white people able to extend compassion to other living beings? If veganism is the notion that we, as humans, can choose plant-based diets (while also clothing and entertaining ourselves without exploitation), as a way of contesting the so-called need for violence toward animals, then are we saying that only white people are capable of understanding this connection? If veganism is concerned with the environmental devastation caused by conventional food systems, then are we saying that only white people can be concerned with the effects this system is having on our planet? Obviously, the answer to all of these questions is no; but we have to ask these questions in order to remind ourselves that veganism does not belong to white people.

Uplifting Our Own

When my colleague Liz Ross and I embarked on creating the *People of Color: Animal Rights, Advocacy and Food Justice* conference, it was because we were tired of having to truck through dense whiteness before we could talk about veganism from the perspective of People of Color. In fact, our decision to create this conference came after attending the only talk on "diversity" that took place at the yearly Animal Rights Conference and being profoundly disappointed by the presentation of what was supposed to be an "inclusive" discussion. The conversation was so shallow and privileged that it was very difficult to understand how we could, or would ever, fit into this movement. Our solution: create our own space.

However, we did not want to create a space where we reproduced whiteness by centering it in our work. In other words, our conference was not intended to be a space where, yet again, the constant focus was on the ways in which white people have dominated the vegan "movement." Nor did we want to do what is now so common in the mainstream movement- the tokenization of PoC by white "intersectional" organizations and people in the vegan world. In fact, we simply did not think it was necessary to talk about white people and white veganism at all. Instead, we wanted to create a space where we focused on People of Color: What work were Vegans of Color doing in PoC communities? What were Vegans of Color doing in the world of animal rights? Advocacy? Animal liberation? Food justice? The environment? What critical, theoretical vegan perspectives were out there that we were missing? How could we learn more about vegan activism where PoC experiences were centered? What were non-white vegans in the rest of the world doing? (Let us not forget that another perspective that is constantly centered is the U.S. perspective.) In other words, we did not want to spend time reacting to these white narratives that we all have experienced over and over and over again; we wanted to build and grow our experiences in vegan spaces, which would by default create a counter narrative and further open up diverse spaces within the vegan movement. In the two conferences we held, we were able to learn from so many inspirational vegans of color doing amazing work.

White supremacy is real, but it doesn't have to be the primary motivation for our activism, it does not have be the only lens through which we view the world. When whiteness is centered, we as PoC become exhausted because our experiences become solely focused on fighting whiteness, without being able to draw from any of the energizing richness of focusing, uplifting and celebrating our own people and the work we do to fight for animal liberation.

Veganism Cannot Be A White Thing Because...

Part of challenging the white vegan narrative also comes through an understanding of our own histories. I contend that, for Vegans of Color, an understanding of slavery, colonization, imperialism, exploitation; an understanding of our liberation struggles, of food and the role it has played both as an oppressive force and as a source of power; of movements aimed at securing land rights and environmental justice are all imperative to informing our veganism. When we understand the ways in which "animalization" has been used to craft notions of non-whiteness on a global scale; when we understand how colonization— specifically, the introduction of colonial foods, of which meat was a fundamental part— shaped how we view food and how status in society became and continues to be deeply intertwined with food; when we understand how non-white communities in the "developing" world have resisted colonization through food, through intricate connections with the earth, with plants and with non-human animals; when we become aware of ancient communities and people around the world who practiced what we now know as veganism; when we recover this historical memory then we will begin to understand that mainstream white veganism is only one perspective. It is not our reality, and it is does not dictate how we engage with veganism. It does not dictate how we will fight for the rights of animals.

In contemporary times, when we as PoC understand how the food system continues to enact extreme violence upon non-white communities and the ways in which it maintains systems of intense inequality and the ways in which the abuse of animals has a direct connection to the abuse of PoC, then we understand the relevance of veganism to Communities of Color around the world. Then we will cease to see veganism as a white thing and understand it as a radical political act, necessary for the liberation of animals and our own liberation.

Most importantly, however, is the need to remember that veganism is a movement focused on animal liberation; humans, in general, are not the focus because under human supremacy, we are the oppressors in the human-nonhuman animal relationship. While our oppressions and path towards liberation are tied, we must be careful to not allow human conditions to overrule our focus on the work toward animal liberation within veganism itself. We should ask ourselves always, how much do we know, how much are we learning about the oppression and structural violence against nonhuman animals? What are we doing to fight *that* oppression? If our discussions and our work in the vegan context solely revolve around human issues, serious as they may be, then we have centered the human and have failed other animals.

recentering nonhuman animals

17

2 BREAKING DOWN
MYTHS AND PERCEPTIONS

By Julia Feliz Brueck, Saryta Rodríguez,
and Ayoola M. White

It is understandable why People of Color would hold myths and perceptions that place an unpalatable light upon veganism and animal rights. After all, as in most spaces and movements, whiteness always demands center stage. Because of this, Vegans of Color are seldomly allowed to lead and given a platform – beyond tokenism – to speak about our own views on veganism as they relate to ethics, oppression, and social justice.

As we've discussed so far in the book, however, when we decenter whiteness and begin to understand how our oppressions are tied to nonhuman oppression, it becomes clear that we are all unwilling victims caught under different systems of oppression under the same oppressor. Whiteness pins us against one another, which simply keeps the circle of supremacy alive.

In an effort to continue to decenter whiteness, the following chapter is set up as an F.A.Q. with brief, to-the-point discussions to help dispel specific myths and perceptions often communicated from Communities of Color.

1. Vegans only care about nonhuman animals.

Every movement, from Black Lives Matter to Palestinian Liberation, centers the victims for whom the respective movement is meant to advocate. Within veganism and animal rights, then, it makes sense that vegans center nonhumans, because of the oppressed-oppressor relationship in which vegan humans reject their alleged supremacy over nonhuman animals. However, there is something to be said about mainstream white veganism's insistence in making attempts at advancing animal advocacy by either combating or ignoring other social movements (Ebrahimi 2019). This is not acceptable.

Vegans of Color understand and know what oppression is and what it feels like. We are aware that our oppression is not comparable to nonhuman oppression. We follow a veganism that rejects one more form of supremacy over the most vulnerable and embrace a consistently anti-oppressive stance across all movements towards all beings. Simply put, veganism of color (as opposed to mainstream white-centered veganism) rejects all forms of oppression and supremacy, including systemic power over nonhuman animals. We believe all oppression is wrong and interconnected. A Person of Color who embraces veganism rejects human supremacy as part of a commitment towards justice for all.

The social justice complex has different movements within it, each focused on the respective marginalized community. Veganism of color is but part of this complex in which we ensure that we also address the supremacy and oppression that humans have enforced upon nonhumans. Nonhuman liberation must also be a part of our conversations if we are to truly achieve justice for ourselves and all others. We are not in competition despite it being set up in this way by a system based on white supremacy —one of the ways in which our oppressions are linked.

Cited Works

Ebrahimi, C. (2019). Personal conversation.

2. Veganism is caping for white supremacy.

When we consider that nonhumans have been used as tools to oppress us for centuries *and* decenter whiteness from veganism, it becomes evident that veganism *challenges* white supremacy.

In essence, white mainstream veganism is based on a type of single-issue advocacy that upholds a supremacist pyramid in which nonhumans are still above marginalized people, including People of Color. We know how often you have probably heard from white vegans that our oppression does not matter, that it has been resolved, or that it comes second to nonhuman oppression. Whiteness and the inability (refusal?) to move beyond single-issue advocacy within the vegan/animal rights movement have created a competition between marginalized human groups and nonhumans— with whiteness at the very top. Through this hierarchical relationship, nonhumans are yet again used as tools of oppression over the most marginalized, including People of Color. They are used to silence People of Color, including Vegans of Color. How? Since nonhumans are unable to talk back, this makes them easier targets to favor in a bid to avoid accountability for white supremacy, while allowing white vegans to benefit from saviorism. In essence, mainstream white veganism makes white vegans "feel good" while doing the bare minimum within the social justice spectrum, since the majority do not address the root issues preventing communities from accessing veganism (but still condemn those communities).

Meanwhile, Vegans of Color reject speciesism, acknowledge colonialism and its effects, are aware of the interconnections between one another's oppressions, and understand that activism can never be one sided or led by the most privileged. We live, breathe, and exist in a world in which systemic oppression is a given for Black and Brown bodies. Activism, for us, isn't about feeling good. It's about survival.

We know that any reproducing or supporting any form of supremacy, regardless of the species, is merely choosing to continue the very cycle that keeps us bound to systemic oppression.

3. Veganism is not cruelty-free.

First and foremost, we get it. THIS IS TRUE! We Vegans of Color readily concede this point; however, this is unrelated to veganism itself, since *human and nonhuman exploitation can be found within both plant-based agriculture **and** within the animal agriculture industry.* Originally, the term "cruelty-free" was embraced by some animal rights activists as a way to differentiate between products that either contained nonhuman biproducts or had been tested on nonhumans, and those that did not and had not. However, many of us understand— and more people are realizing every day— that producing a product without these qualities may still cause irreparable harm to humans (workers, populations displaced by farming, etc.). In embracing veganism, we seek to reduce the cruelty committed against both nonhumans and human workers.

The chapter "Making Connections 'In the Name of

Food'" in the book *Food Justice: A Primer* (Rodríguez 2018) outlined the ways in which animal agriculture is tied to horrific cruelty against People of Color, which make up the majority of its workers, as well as the interconnections between racism, food justice, and nonhuman animal exploitation. From unsafe working conditions, to the exploitation of undocumented migrants and refugees, to psychological distress from repetitive violence witnessed and inflicted by workers on nonhuman animals in slaughterhouses, to environmental racism in which our own communities experience the worst effects from animal-agriculture-caused pollutants, there are myriad examples of the ways in which *veganism takes an active stance against cruelty to our own communities.*

Adding to this, rejecting animal agriculture means to recognize and take an active stance against the atrocities currently facing Indigenous people and natural areas, such as the Amazon rainforest, as well as an ineffective food production system in which millions go hungry.

The intensive farming of livestock has contributed to the detriment of wild areas and resources due to their unsustainable high demand for water and feed, as well as the high output of waste (Secretariat of the Convention for Biological Diversity 2008). Adding to the need for intense crop production is a dependency on monocultures focused on the agriculture of soybeans— but not for human consumption (Kryda 2014). The majority of soybeans and other cereals are currently used as a high-protein feed for livestock, including pigs, poultry, and grain-dependent cow farming across

Europe, the U.S., and Canada (Steinfeld et al. 1997).

Incredibly, the U.N.'s Food and Agriculture Organization (FAO) reports that, "Twenty-six percent of the planet's ice-free land is used for livestock grazing and 33 percent of croplands are used for livestock feed production." Livestock feed crop production takes up one-third of the world's arable land already (Bland 2012). The FAO warns that, "With rising incomes in the developing world, demand for animal products will continue to surge; 74 percent for meat, 58 percent for dairy products and 500 percent for eggs. Meeting increasing demand is a major sustainability challenge (Food and Agriculture Organization 2012)".

A decade ago, Cornell ecologist David Pimentel boldly proclaimed that, "If all the grain currently fed to livestock in the United States were consumed directly by people, the number of people who could be fed would be nearly 800 million." (Cornell Chronicle 1997). Later, we find that nearly the same number of people remain hungry. The FAO affirms that, "Globally, there is enough cropland to feed 9 billion in 2050 if the 40 percent of all crops produced today for feeding animals were used directly for human consumption..." (Food and Agriculture Organization 2012). Going back to sustainability and its importance, Duncan Williamson, WWF food policy manager, points out that, "A staggering 60% of global biodiversity loss is down to the food we eat. We know a lot of people are aware that a meat-based diet has an impact on water and land, as well as causing greenhouse gas emissions, but few know the biggest issue of all comes from the crop-based feed the animals eat

(Smithers 2017)."

Even though veganism is not inherently cruelty-free, non-veganism is tied to even *more* systems of oppression that disproportionately affect Communities of Color. A shift towards the rejection of nonhuman animal exploitation is a step towards ensuring that we also stand up for our own communities.

Cited Works

Bland, A. (2012). Is the Livestock Industry Destroying the Planet? *Smithsonian.com*: https://www.smithsonianmag.com/travel/is-the-livestock-industry-destroying-the-planet-11308007

Cornell Chronicle (1997). U.S. could feed 800 million people with grain that livestock eat, Cornell ecologist advises animal scientists. *Cornell.edu*: http://news.cornell.edu/stories/1997/08/us-could-feed-800-million-people-grain-livestock-eat

Food and Agricultural Organization (2012). Livestock and Landscapes. *Sustainability Pathways*: http://www.fao.org/docrep/018/ar591e/ar591e.pdf

Kryda, M. (2014). Soya – a Problematic Animal Feed. *Agricultural and Rural Convention*: http://www.arc2020.eu/soya-a-problematic-animal-feed/

Rodríguez, S. (2018). *Food Justice: A Primer*. Sanctuary

Publishers.

Secretariat of the Convention on Biological Diversity
(2008). *Biodiversity and Agriculture: Safeguarding
Biodiversity and Securing Food for the World*. Montreal,
56 pages: https://www.cbd.int/doc/bioday/2008/ibd-
2008-booklet-en.pdf

Smithers, Rebecca (2017). Vast Animal-feed Crops to
Satisfy Our Meat Needs are   Destroying Planet. *The
Guardian*: https://www.theguardian.com/environment/
2017/oct/05/vast-animal-feed-crops-meat-needs-
destroying-planet

Steinfeld, H., de Haan, C. and Blackburn, H. (1997).
*Beyond Production Systems in Livestock-Environment
Interactions.* Food and Agriculture Organization.

4. It's too expensive and not accessible for all PoC.

Accessibility is a root issue that needs to be
addressed with regards to plant foods and vegan
products for those that are less privileged. However,
accessibility due to economic hardship does not only
apply to veganism or plant-based foods or items when
we consider that, in the U.S. alone, 12.3% of the overall
population lives in poverty (Fontenot et al. 2018).

Veganism itself is not expensive. In fact, surveys have
shown that *most vegans are not wealthy and come from
below-average household incomes* (VRG 2015), while

recently a study published in the Journal of Hunger and Environmental Nutrition revealed that meatless diets are actually cheaper and healthier (Flynn and Schiff 2015). While processed meat alternatives and specialty items can be costly, they are not requirements for healthy plant-based diets or in making other vegan choices.

When it comes to accessibility, our role should be to do as much as we can, because we are privileged enough to have access to alternatives, towards working against intersecting oppressions, aligning our ethics with our actions, rejecting human supremacy, improving environmental health, and more. Marginalized groups should never be used as an excuse when they depend on us to do the most that we can as we work towards liberation.

It is also important to note that the fact that a particular group of people might not be able to go vegan right now does not mean they will never be able to do so and thus, should not be used as an excuse not to go vegan. For instance, some people with unrelated roots or ancestry in more isolated destinations, such as Alaska, will use these areas as an example of a place where getting enough calories through a plant-based diet is not currently feasible for most people and "...therefore, veganism can't work on a global scale; and, if it can't work for everybody, why should anybody bother to adopt it?" Rather than dismissing veganism on these grounds as people not even from these communities or shaming people who live in such regions for not just going vegan "for the animals," as many white vegans do, we should all aim to develop technologies and processes such as hydroponic growing, which, while still too young and too expensive to be considered accessible, hold great promise for increased accessibility to fresh produce worldwide in the future. Any vegan who genuinely wants the world to go vegan should support such efforts, while non-vegans who live in industrialized nations with moderate climates (such as the mainland U.S.) have no business using Alaskans or any other population as an excuse to continue eating nonhuman animals when they themselves clearly do not have to do so.

Cited Works

Flynn, M. and Schiff, A. (2015). Economical Healthy Diets (2012): Including Lean Animal Protein Costs More Than Using Extra Virgin Olive Oil. *Journal of Hunger and Environmental Nutrition*. Vol 10: 4, 467-482.

Fontenot, K., Semega, J., and Kollar, M. (2018). *Income and Poverty in the United States: 2017*. United States Census Bureau: https://www.census.gov/library/publications/2018/demo/p60-263.html

Stahler, Chris (2015). *How Often Do Americans Eat Vegetarian Meals? And How Many Adults in the U.S. Are Vegetarian?* VRG.org: http://www.vrg.org/blog/2015/05/29/how-often-do-americans-eat-vegetarian-meals-and-how-many-adults-in-the-u-s-are-vegetarian-2/

5. Veganism is a consumer boycott, and consumer boycotts are not effective.

Veganism is an ethical and justice-based stance against the exploitation and oppression of nonhuman animals under human supremacy (speciesism). While boycotts are clearly part of veganism in that they reject oppression where possible in everyday choices, which is tied to how we spend our money as consumers, embracing veganism and including other animals' rights in our fight towards liberation for all is not merely a consumer boycott. In addition, whether consumer boycotts are effective or not depends on how they are done, the available resources, and the reasons behind them. Plant-based foods and vegan products have become widely available because of consumers. Regardless, when it comes to consumerism, we will not achieve our end goals under a capitalism-based system, which is still dependent on the exploitation of the marginalized. Therefore, veganism does not and cannot hinge on its economic impact; it is a broader philosophy for living, a belief system and the staunch rejection of a belief system all at once. It involves reimagining society, and, in such a society, boycotts would not even be necessary because there would no longer be companies or stocks or money of any kind. To examine veganism through the lens of abstention— of merely not buying things— misses the point.

6. We should achieve liberation for oppressed humans before advocating for nonhuman rights.

Although animal exploitation and oppression of humans are by no means equivalent, they are linked. When racists refer to People of Color as "animals" or treat People of Color like "animals," this is not to say that other animals are bad in and of themselves. Statements and actions such as these are acknowledgements of the reality that *humans treat nonhuman animals in violent ways and that this violence is largely accepted and excused.* If this were not the case, comparing People of Color to animals would make about as much sense as comparing them to fire hydrants or trees.

The ideological frameworks that excuse the exploitation of nonhuman animals often extend to the oppression of humans. For example, consider the idea that some lives are superior to others, or the notion that a perceived lack of intelligence justifies the denial of bodily autonomy. Why, and how, is this justified? Cognitive dissonance is the discomfort that keeps us from acknowledging an opposing value or idea that contradicts our deep-seated beliefs (Festinger 1957). This form of psychological distress is necessary to entertain ideological frameworks that enable us to take part in the obviously violent oppression of others and thus, taints the possibility for true liberation of either ourselves or nonhuman animals.

A significant characteristic of capitalism is that it frames lives, bodies, and the things those bodies produce as commodities. This phenomenon victimizes both humans and non-human animals— though, of course, not in the same ways. Full liberation from capitalism, imperialism, and other oppressive structures cannot occur if so-called liberators are caging, killing, or otherwise exploiting sentient beings. Because of this, it is imperative that we address all forms of liberation at once in order to break down interconnecting structures that have power over us all.

Cited Works

Festinger, L. (1957). *A Theory of Cognitive Dissonance.* California: Stanford University Press.

7. We should let white people worry about nonhuman animals because People of Color have their own problems to deal with towards addressing our own liberation.

While People of Color absolutely have our own struggles and fight towards our own liberation, we cannot ignore the fact that, even if you don't personally like or care about nonhuman animals, their exploitation does negatively impact human beings— especially People of Color. Ranching and other more land-intensive forms of animal agriculture often encroach upon Indigenous territory. Farms with livestock are more likely to exist near Communities of Color, meaning that fecal matter and other waste products pollute nearby land and water. In turn, corporate farms often collaborate with town legislatures to ensure that people who live nearby are not allowed to take legal action against such pollution (Hellerstein 2017). Slaughterhouses— which mainly employ immigrant People of Color, many of whom are vulnerable as a result of being undocumented— have high rates of PTSD and physical health problems (Rodríguez 2018).

Most urgently, since scientists have warned that we have but a few years before we reach a point of no return with regards to the impact of climate change (Watts 2018), we must recognize that animal agriculture has a significant impact on its hastening. Study after study has shown that People of Color are significantly more at risk than white people as the impacts of climate change intensify (Fischer 2009).

Regardless of the impacts that nonhuman oppression has on People of Color, when we think about our hand in the exploitation of others, it is also our responsibility to address it and to eliminate it. Nonhuman animals farmed or hunted for food, animals used as test subjects, those used for clothing and entertainment, as well as the wildlife fighting the effects of human-caused environmental degradation, fight just as hard for their lives as we would if our lives were in danger. Survival is not unique to human communities and neither is the right to live free from harm, exploitation, abuse, and death.

Cited Works

Fischer, D. (2009). Climate change hits poor hardest in U.S. *Scientific American*: https://www.scientificamerican .com /article/climate-change-hits-poor-hardest

Hellerstein, E. (2017). The N.C. Senate overrides Cooper's HB 467 veto, Hog-Farm-Protection Bill is law. *IndyWeek*: https://indyweek.com/news/archives/n.c.-senate-overrides-cooper-s-hb-467-veto-hog-farm-protection-bill-law

Rodríguez, S. (2018) *Food Justice: A Primer*. Sanctuary Publishers.

Watts, J. (2018). We Have 12 Years to Limit Climate Change Catastrophe, Warns UN. *The Guardian*: https://www.theguardian.com/environment/2018/oct/08/global-warming-must-not-exceed-15c-warns-landmark-un-report

8. Consuming, wearing, and using other animals for entertainment is part of our culture and traditions.

This is no doubt true, since this is the case in nearly every culture. However, the problem with this argument against veganism and animal rights is that it assumes that certain practices can be deemed ethical as long as they hold some cultural significance (Ebrahimi 2019).

If we look through each of our culture's history, we would be readily able to identify a plethora of actions and perceptions held by society that the oppressive majority no longer finds acceptable, including some that laws have been passed to prohibit child labor, dog fighting, human slavery, etc. Current cultural values, therefore, <u>cannot be</u> used as a metric for ethical <u>behavior</u>, and in the case of animal rights and veganism, cultural significance does not deem something justifiable when we have moved forward enough to acknowledge that our practices against other living beings are exploitative and oppressive.

As People of Color, our history is often tied to colonialism, which made large-scale exploitation of our resources, environment, and people acceptable through white supremacist ideology. <u>Colonialism imported practices</u> such as fur farming and livestock farming operations, among others. Even many of our foods have been impacted by colonial influences, <u>making many forms of nonhuman animal</u> exploitation *not* inherently "<u>cultural" to us</u>. For instance, Black vegan Christopher Sebastian McJetters (2019) explained that, "While humans have used fur as protection against cold for centuries, the widespread breeding of animals as textiles is traced back to European markets, and the earliest records of breeding mink for fur in North America were in Canada, circa 1865...Fast forward to today, and most of the world's farmed fur is produced by European farmers."

Another example is nonhumans used for sport. Similarly, <u>cockfighting</u> in Puerto Rico and <u>bullfighting in</u> Mexico were <u>traditions</u> established merely 500 years ago— by <u>Spanish colonizers</u>. These forms of nonhuman exploitation are not only *not* traditional to our communities but also, ironically, often highlight double standards placed on forms of nonhuman animal exploitation that were part of societies *before* the arrival of Europeans, which are deemed "less than" because they are practiced by those most marginalized through colonialism.

We can extend the same colonialist connections when we consider some of the foods that we now consider staples. In the book *Food Justice: A Primer* (2018), Saryta Rodríguez noted that while following Columbus's arrival, Europe profited from the discovery of plant foods in America, "America in turn received goats, horses, chickens, cows, and other nonhuman animals." Rodríguez further explained that:

> This not only led to a boom of animal agriculture in the US among white settlers, but the introduction of horses to America also resulted in many Native American tribes shifting from an (often plant-based) agricultural society to a nomadic society reliant on hunting. Not only did these changes result in myriad injustices against nonhuman animals, as they were exploited as both food and transportation, but they also wreaked havoc on Caribbean natives— human and nonhuman alike. Native nonhuman populations in the Caribbean suffered, while conucos, plots of land managed by indigenous peoples for sustenance, were damaged.

A Ph.D. in Philosophy focused on the history and philosophy of science, animal studies, feminist philosophy, bioethics and social theory, David M. Peña-Guzmán (2018) further broke-down the importance of knowing the connections between what we eat in the now and colonialism in an effort to emphasize the political consciousness of veganism to People of Color:

> *Our very eating habits, then, are reflections of a colonial event that very much still is a living force in our present. In how we eat and what we eat, we play and replay the very source of our collective trauma. The dinner table as colonial and neo-colonial reenactment.*

Dr. Peña-Guzmán continued,

> *Combating colonialism in the way we eat requires us to act on several levels: by reflecting on the ways in which many of our contemporary dietary practices are not really "ours" but have instead been forced on us by external actors too diffuse to name; by reclaiming the foods of our ancestors, those pre-Colombian staples that so many of us know about in the abstract but haven't woven into our everyday life; and by facing up to the fact that our modern-day eating habits perpetuate the violence of which colonialism is only one expression—by sacrificing living beings for the sake of human gusto.*

This discussion has barely begun touching upon the surface of the influences that white supremacy forced upon our relationship with nonhumans and each other because most of us will have similar but very different relationships and oppressions with colonialism and white supremacy, particularly due to anti-blackness and anti-indigeneity.

center & margins Anzaldua
proximity to whiteness/privilege

Can you think of ways colonial influences oppressed your own community, and how this oppression included the use of nonhuman animals? As you explore this issue, you will begin to see the layers of interconnections between our oppression and how nonhumans are used to keep us oppressed (and *have* been used to oppress us). The forced implementation of lines drawn between "us" and "them" will become clearer: the closer we embrace and resemble whiteness through acceptance and assimilation, the more favorably we, People of Color, are seen under our white supremacist infused societies. Therefore, when we reject nonhuman exploitation and traditions rooted in colonialism, we *add* to the work needed to undo white supremacy itself.

It must be noted that even People of Color must let other People of Color address their own communities when it comes to traditions and customs. Respecting this, however, does not mean supporting nonhuman exploitation, since Communities of Color are defined by much more than the forms of exploitation in which they partake. As Vegans of Color, our aim is to address these issues within our own communities and learn from, as well as raise the voices of, one another without speaking over our own issues. We must also be conscious to center the most marginalized within our own communities and truly listen so that we may address root issues that prevent us from moving forward.

Cited Works

Ebrahimi, C. (2019). Personal conversation.

McJetters, C. (2019). *Tiffany Haddish Protesting Police Violence with Fur is the Embodiment of Weaponized Oppression*. ChristopherSebastian.info: https://www.christophersebastian.info/single-post/2019/01/01/Tiffany-Haddish-protesting-police-violence-with-fur-is-the-embodiment-of-weaponized-oppression

Peña-Guzmán, D. M. (2018). Anti-Colonial Food Politics: A Case Study. In *Action from Mexico*. Faunalytics.org: https://faunalytics.org/anti-colonial-food-politics-a-case-study-in-action-from-mexico

Rodríguez, S. *Food Justice: A Primer*. Sanctuary Publishers.

9. Aligning veganism as a liberation movement justifies white supremacist notions that equate Black people and other Communities of Color to nonhuman animals as a basis for oppression.

In their book, Black vegan theorists Aph and Syl Ko explained that the line between "us" (humans) and "them" (nonhuman animals) is an idea founded on cis-male whiteness. The authors propose that if we finally oppose the idea that nonhumans are opposite to humans, including ourselves, we will begin to break down the cycle of oppression placed upon us under white supremacy (Ko 2017).

In essence, aligning veganism as a liberation movement is not what justifies white supremacist ideology. It's the actual divide in which we, Black people and other People of Color (and other marginalized groups) are animalized and automatically seen as "less than" through a supremacist hierarchy which places different values on us based on closeness to those at the top – human, white, cis, male, and able-bodied. Veganism does not equate Black people specifically, or any other specific group of humans, with nonhuman animals; it recognizes that *all* humans and nonhuman animals fall under the biological umbrella of "animals." In this way, Vegans of Color reject the white supremacist narrative and embrace a truly non-hierarchical vision of society.

Cited Works

Ko, Aph and Syl (2017). *Aphro-ism: Essays on Pop Culture, Feminism, and Black Veganism from Two Sisters.* Lantern Books.

10. Vegans will advocate for issues that affect nonhuman animals' rights while neglecting efforts to support, organize, and advocate for human rights.

Mainstream white veganism has failed in its effort to ensure it does not exclude marginalized people and add to their oppression. As Vegans of Color, however, we propose something different. We challenge People of

Color to decenter whiteness completely from their view of veganism. White folks merely named the concept because they had a platform and the privilege to focus on taking a stance against nonhuman animal exploitation, while Black and Brown bodies were fighting for their right to live. (It is also worth noting that there were some populations of color who lived a vegan or near-vegan lifestyle long before the term was invented). While our communities are still fighting for many of the same goals and rights— including the mere recognition of our personhood— ethics, morality, and the fight against all oppression (including that in which we have a hand in, as discussed by Dr. Alvarez in the Introduction) are not white concepts. Veganism does not belong to whiteness.

It is also important to recognize that while there are only so many hours in a day and we are exhausted from our own battles, it is possible to be active in advocating for more than one population at once. This is something Vegans of Color attempt to do as we work to dismantle all forms of oppression consistently, including our own. Choosing to embrace a consistently anti-oppressive stance across the board helps us all to break down hierarchies one by one, collectively. This makes it easier to break down multiple forms of supremacy by exposing the flaws and interconnected roots of oppression inherent in *all* hierarchies. Choosing to include veganism in our social justice work takes nothing away from the work also being done for specific groups of humans – and vice versa. Ultimately, it is essential that we strive to blur the lines between our "work" or "activism" and our *lives*— the way in which we conduct ourselves and the choices we make every single day. In so doing, we can choose to not only advocate for on occasion but also to actually *live* in a way that advocates for humans and nonhumans alike— without ever having to choose between them.

3 PERSPECTIVES
from
Vegans of Color

The Paradox of (In)Consistency in Anti-Oppression

By Doreen Akiyo Yomoah

I'm relatively new to veganism, but I've been a card-carrying Social Justice Warrior (SJW) before SJW became a Twitter epithet. I'm a Black woman, born in Ghana to Ghanaian parents, who spent her childhood and adolescence in highly-developed countries. As a result, as a Black, African woman, I've tended to occupy a space between privileged and oppressed— what Kimberlé Crenshaw coined "intersectionality." While living at a cross-section of identities is hardly unique, there are some peculiarities of being an immigrant child, particularly one whose parents moved you from a developing economy to a developed one (or two).

For example, while navigating racism, white supremacy, patriarchy, and anti-immigrant sentiments is part of my daily existence, so is having access to resources like education, constant running water and electricity, effective and efficient transportation, and a range of healthcare services that are available relatively quickly (although not necessarily affordably). In many cases, these living standards were built on the exploitation of countries like Ghana— countries that were subjected to colonialism and are now subjected to neocolonialism.

If we want to be part of a social justice movement that advocates for *consistent* anti-oppression, we need to be willing to examine our own biases and privileges—

and, ultimately, to advocate for our own surrender of them. On the one hand, that means confronting our speciesism, which most people were raised with, and ending our participation in the exploitation of non-human animals. On the other, it means interrogating our own prejudices as well as our participation in systems that actively exploit other humans. Without understanding how the exploitation of humans and non-human animals are intertwined, how can we dismantle oppressive systems?

Ghana, for example, imports meat from countries as far away as Brazil (I used to facilitate this as part of my job while living in Ghana). This system is exploitative from start to finish: from the animals who are raised and slaughtered in terrible conditions for human consumption, to the people in Brazil who have to work in these terrible conditions, to the people in Ghana whose local food systems are being decimated by the import of these products.

So, for those of us non-white vegans who have chosen to live, to the best of our ability, in a way that is as anti-oppressive as possible yet also reside in countries where we experience oppression (but also privilege, by virtue of being there), it *is* justified when non-vegan People of Color point out that this shouldn't be the end point of our activism. What do we owe our family and fellow People of Color in the South? Does it stop at making individual choices not to consume or support the exploitation of both human and non-human animals? Or do we have a responsibility to do more?

I was not born vegan, and there are, no doubt, many ways to fight colonialism and neocolonialism in addition to adopting vegan politics. Black PoC, no matter where we are, experience anti-blackness; yet it is more noticeable to those of us in majority non-Black countries, simply because of the optics. Our Black family and friends who *don't* live in Europe, the Americas, Asia, or the Pacific may not recognize the oppression that they face as being rooted in anti-blackness due to the simple fact that their day-to-day lives don't include micro-level racial harassment or discrimination, the way they do for so many of us in the diaspora.

However, the macro-level policy decisions— from colonialism, neocolonialism, and structural adjustment policies to market-level decisions, such as extraction of natural resources and importation of finished products— all contribute to economic, environmental and social injustices we face, especially those of us in Africa and the Caribbean. Animal agriculture and exploitation across the globe add to these very injustices that we must dismantle.

Even if you haven't made the connection yet, or don't *want* to make the connection yet (and this is no judgement on anyone; I didn't become an ethical vegan until I was in my thirties), our oppression; the oppression of non-white people; the oppression of anyone who has ever experienced, on a systemic level, what it's like to not be the decision makers of their own bodies...These cannot be separated from the oppression of non-human animals.

I'm not trying to convince you that the Atlantic slave trade and institutional racism, colonialism, legally sanctioned rape, or other obviously horrific forms of oppression against humans are *the same* as what we humans do to animals, because no form of oppression is identical to another form of oppression, even if there are clear overlaps and even if one person can experience multiple forms simultaneously. However, in exactly the same way that we don't say that racism and homophobia, for example, are "the same," we can still draw parallels between them. They both rely on a hegemonic understanding of who is deserving of full human rights, and who is a second-class citizen, based on nothing more than historical and systemic power hoarding.

Humans are not "the same" as pigs, who are not the same as dogs, who are not the same as llamas; but this does not mean that humans, based on the accident of who we were born as, have the right to use other beings without their consent, for our own ends. We would be remiss to ignore the fact that **the same class of people who created (and benefit from) white supremacy and capitalism as we know it (and believe it to be inherently just and true, rather than constructed by them) are the same class of people who created (and benefit from) the speciesism that many of us have come to accept as an inherent truth.**

Vegan activists of color have already started doing important work towards advocating for a more just world— one that includes racial, gender, environmental, and economic justice, and animal liberation. While it is not our place, as vegans, to tell people what to put in their bodies, ending racism and anti-blackness means we must recognize that the oppression of non-human animals is tied up in the oppression of Black people. People like Aph Ko and Dr. Breeze Harper, to name only two of the brilliant vegan scholars of color out there, have already done important work deconstructing the links between oppression of people of color and oppression of animals.

So, what's next? How do we keep combating the injustices that affect us all? How do we hold ourselves accountable beyond the Global North? We make the choice to adopt consistency in our anti-oppression work and use what we know to amplify the voices of people in the South who are advocating for their own rights, such as for ownership over their land its resources, which are being exploited to the detriment and even deaths of people on their land. Many people in the South have already made the connection between their *(our)* oppression and the oppression of non-human animals. Even if you're not there, as you work towards understanding the interconnections and injustices that People of Color face globally, you will discover that one of the largest contributors is mass agriculture and its documented and impossible-to-ignore harmful effects.

According to a report released by the UN Intergovernmental Panel on Climate Change (IPCC) in October 2018, if we don't halt climate change within the next twelve years, we're all doomed. What the headlines fail to mention is that we've already allowed hundreds of thousands of Black and Brown people to perish from climate-change-related effects as a result of our negligence in tackling the issue.

We can spread awareness of the dangers of concentrated animal feeding operations, of poaching and leather tanning to the environment and to people, and how in our disregard for the lives and autonomy of other species, we're destroying their habitats and our own. We cannot live on this Earth if we cannot coexist peacefully with its other inhabitants, whether it's people who are different from us, or they're species that are different from our own. We can try to live by example every day of our lives. We can advocate to our governments on the local and national levels to protect the people who do the dirty work so that we can enjoy our fur-lined hoods and steak dinners in dangerous conditions, even more so than the people who do this same work in industrialized countries. Because, as author and activist Emma Lazarus once said, "Until we are all free, none of us are free."

Ethical Consumption under Capitalism?

By Shahada Chowdhury

What was initially meant to be a criticism of capitalism is now commonly used to justify over-consumption, to the detriment and complete disregard of the working class and all of the non-human animals who are directly or indirectly harmed in the production of commodities. The statement "There is no ethical consumption under capitalism" tends to get thrown around whenever people begin to look at the processes behind producing the commodities we consume and the effects they have on workers and non-human animals. The means of production are the technology, tools, resources and facilities needed to produce the goods that workers create. Capitalism is the economic and political system in which the world operates, and it is one in which the means of production are privately owned for the purposes of amassing profit for a group of people known as the bourgeoisie.

Wealth— and, subsequently, profit— does not come into existence on its own; Earth's natural resources, which are also mostly privately owned, are utilized and processed by workers to create goods. Most goods produced are owned neither by the workers who produce them nor the people from whom the resources were appropriated. Capitalism is fundamentally rooted in the exploitation of labor and the private ownership of the means of production. Ethical consumption is the attempt to make mindful consumer choices to reduce an individual's impact on the environment, the exploitation of workers, and, if they happen to be vegan, the exploitation of non-human animals.

Originally, the phrase "There is no ethical consumption under capitalism" highlighted the fact that with all labor being exploited by capitalists, no consumption under capitalism could ever be regarded as ethical. Ironically, this fact is often subverted to *reinforce* capitalism by people who have an interest in maintaining their consumer behaviors. It is not only the bourgeoisie, also known as the capitalist class, that uphold this system, but also (typically) those who can afford to be effective consumers; this is reflected in the general apathy and even disdain held by such people for workers and migrants from poorer nations. Precarious and disenfranchised workers— who are disproportionately from the global south and, therefore, BIPoC (Black, Indigenous, and People of Color)— are hyper-exploited in what is offhandedly described as "low-skill work" to produce consumer goods. Additionally, in the race to amass as much profit as possible, nonhuman animals are exploited and killed at an exponential rate. It is important to note that the agricultural revolution occurred in Britain (mid-17th to late 19th century), whose economy relied on slavery and colonialism; the practice of intensive farming was first developed in the 20th century and has only become more "efficient" at the expense of sentient lives and the environment ever since.

Imperialism, as described by Lenin, is the highest stage of capitalism. In the earlier stages of capitalism, free-market competition drove the economy. This kind of freedom, of course, was upheld over the freedom of colonized people in their right to self-determination. Imperialism develops out of free-market competition. Simply put, "Imperialism is the monopoly stage of capitalism" (Lenin, 1916). As the bourgeoisie compete amongst themselves for the ownership of production and the accumulation of capital, both capital and the means of production inevitably become concentrated in the hands of a few. Lenin explains that capital from industry and capital from banks merge to become "finance capital," which is then exported to under-developed territories/nations for the purposes of further exploitation and search for profits. This development of capitalism to such a stage means that a system of monopoly domination is what drives the economy; it is no longer free-market competition.

Imperialist nations assert political power and economic domination over non-imperialist nations by means of exporting finance capital, installing governments against the will of the people, and using military power to suppress liberation movements. The US, UK and the EU bloc are fundamentally imperialist; they all have a neo-colonial relationship with most non-imperial nations. Kwame Nkrumah explains that neo-colonialism is where once colonized territories/nations are still economically dependent on— and, therefore, have their political policy controlled by— imperialists, all the while *appearing* to be independent states (Nkrumah, 1965). Furthermore, the US, Canada, Israel, and Australia are examples of *settler colonial states*. Colonizers seize and occupy land that is already inhabited by natives/Indigenous people and commit acts of genocide, such as destroying subsistence farms with the intent to kill them through starvation and engaging in outright massacres and displacement.

For example:

- After his "discovery of the new world" in 1492, Christopher Columbus returned to the Caribbean islands the following year with a fleet to subjugate, enslave and exterminate the native peoples. "Columbus's programs reduced Taino numbers from as many as eight million at the outset of his regime to about three million in 1496. Perhaps 100,000 were left by the time of the governor's departure. His policies, however, remained, with the result that by 1514 the Spanish census of the island showed barely 22,000 Indians remaining alive. In 1542, only two hundred were recorded. Thereafter, they were considered extinct, as were Indians throughout the Caribbean Basin, an aggregate population which totalled more than fifteen million at the point of first contact with the Admiral of the Ocean Sea, as Columbus was known (Churchill, 1994)."

- The seventh president of the United States, Andrew Jackson, signed the Indian Removal Act into law in 1830, which allowed the "resettlement" (displacement) of Indigenous people in Mississippi from the land they lived in to unsettled land in the west of the state.

Approximately 100 Cherokee leaders signed the Treaty of New Echota, in which they were promised provisions and benefits in return for relinquishing all land east of the Mississippi River. This was used to justify the forcible removal of almost 17,000 Cherokees in 1838. "An estimated 4,000 died from hunger, exposure and disease. The journey became a cultural memory as the 'trail where they cried' for the Cherokees and other removed tribes. Today it is widely remembered by the general public as the 'Trail of Tears' (Cherokee Nation 2019)."

- *Settler colonialism is an ongoing process,* so long as the settler/native relationship exists. The settler colonial regimes against natives/Indigenous peoples operate to this day, not only in the US and Canada, but also in Palestine. Among the daily injustices of being second-class citizens, Palestinians in the West Bank continue to have their lands encroached by settlers— mainly through house demolitions, which have happened since the Six-Day War in 1967, and attacks on farms. "In just over two months, from the beginning of May to 7 July 2018, B'Tselem documented 10 instances in which settlers destroyed a total of more than 2,000 trees and grapevines and burned down a barley field and bales of hay (B'Tselem 2018)."

Imperialism does not only affect humans, however; land encroachment by imperialist powers for the purposes of animal agriculture, resource extraction, and trophy hunting are examples of ways non-human animals are also harmed by this system. These practices that only seek to extract profits for a minority, not for the benefit of humans, are driving the sixth mass species extinction. Imperialism exposes the ugly nature of animal agriculture as we develop production to such a stage that *billions* of animals can be bred into existence just to squeeze as much profit out as possible, with absolutely no regard for sentient life.

The definition of speciesism differs depending on who wants to define it. Unfortunately, when defined by single-issue vegans, it is used to dismiss the struggles of marginalize and oppressed people. The issue with defining speciesism as merely human supremacy over animals (and trying to draw equivalence to racism and misogyny from it) is that it dismisses the historical factors in the development of our species in relation to non-human animals and obfuscates the social, political and economic relations we have with each other.

Single-issue vegans see speciesism as the most overriding oppression. as opposed to one of the many forms of oppression that are tied to capitalism, and mistakenly believe that being vegan absolves them of benefiting from speciesism and other kinds of systemic oppression. This reductive, individualist approach is often used to dismiss any form of accountability by white vegans in their role under capitalism, which is inherently white supremacist, patriarchal and speciesist. Historically, as a species, homo sapiens have hunted/domesticated animals for food, clothing and transport; we cannot erase this fact, nor should we use this as means to justify exploitation where exploitation is not necessary. In the present day, many of us live in societies in which the level of production is advanced to the point that we do not have to hunt/farm non-human animals, and one in which the knowledge of thriving without exploiting animals is accessible, even though there are interests that run disinformation campaigns or promote biased research to protect animal agricultural industries (Pippus 2017).

Speciesism, therefore, is the exploitation of non-human animals by humans where exploitation is not necessary for survival.

What is the significance behind imperialism and settler colonialism with regards to speciesism? The endangerment of wild non-human species is a result of colonial aggression, and conservation projects to protect these now-endangered animals become another tool for settlers to occupy land and sever the ties Indigenous/native people have with said land. In the West, for example:

> The model of conservation derived from settler colonialism is predicated on the threat of extermination made possible by the disruption of relationships among beings. In other words, it is the translation of land (rich with dynamic and interlocking relationships) into habitat (situated for the survival of a single or hierarchical set of species). In this sense, conservation is not just about sustaining a place, and its ways and species, or even a species itself, but about

conserving the endurance of the settler colonial project, a way of life that individuates by separation, eliminates through replacement, and sustains through domination (Burow 2017).

The economic and political complexities surrounding our everyday lives are easy to dismiss if one benefits from such injustices and oppression. The reality is that there is no ethical consumption under capitalism because all labor is exploited by the ruling class who profit from it. However, this does not give one free reign over perpetuating or upholding the capitalist system and, therefore, siding with oppressive forces. The phrase was meant to engage critical thought towards economic production— not to dismiss it.

Capitalism is inherently destructive and oppressive; it keeps the majority systematically disadvantaged, working to produce wealth that is then appropriated by the bourgeoisie, while destroying ecosystems and the environment in the process. There can be no liberation for BIPoC/women/workers (it is important to remember that these groups of people *are not mutually exclusive*) under capitalism. It is imperative that we address these issues through organized, politicized boycotts and resistance to capitalism. We must show solidarity with people currently resisting colonialism/imperialism globally, whether they are currently pursuing animal rights or not, while creating the conditions that allow people to engage with the concept of consistent anti-oppression.

Cited Works

B'Tselem (2018). Settler Violence: Absence of Law Enforcement. *btselem.org*:
https://www.btselem.org/settler_violence/20180802_se ttlers_destroy_2000_palestinian_owned_trees

Burow, P. (2017). Wildlife Conservation and Settler Colonialism in the North American West. *Anthropology and Environmental Society*: https://aesengagement. wordpress.com/2017/03/28/wildlife-conservation-and-settler-colonialism-in-the-north-american-west/

Cherokee Nation (2019). A Brief History of the Trail of Tears. *Cheerokee.org*. Accessed January 20, 2019: https://cherokee.org/About-The-Nation/History/Trail-of-Tears/A-Brief-History-of-the-Trail-of-Tears

Churchill, W. (1994). Columbus and the Beginning of Genocide in the "New World". In *Indians Are Us? Culture and Genocide in Native North America*. Common Courage Press, Maine.

Lenin, V. (1916). *Imperialism, the Highest Stage of Capitalism.* Progress Publishers, Moscow.

Nkrumah, K. (1965). *Neo-Colonialism, the Last Stage of imperialism*. Panaf Books, U.K.

Pippus, A. (2017). Dairy Industry Funds Research Saying Dairy Is Good; Researcher Denies Documented Ties. *HuffingtonPost.com*: https://www.huffingtonpost.com/ entry/dairy-industry-funds-research-saying-dairy-is-good_us_

The Movement of Time, Culture, and Perceptions: Growing up in Borikén

By Julia Feliz Brueck

Some vegans of color find their path towards veganism through plant-based eating for health or environmentalism – just a couple of the benefits of a diet that is part of a movement centered on justice. Although my background is in science and I hold an M.Sc. in conservation ecology, my story is a bit different.

I was born and raised on the island of Puerto Rico – known as Borikén before colonialism. I have wonderful memories of growing up with my mother and my great-aunt, Luma. Raised by a hard-working single mom, I spent many summers crafting and taking bus trips with my great-aunt to Old San Juan. My weekends were spent with my mom at home, the beach, or at several of the playgrounds in the metropolitan area. Both of these strong presences in my life were the first to introduce me to companion animals.

The first-ever nonhumans sharing my home space were fishes, budgies, and a Guinea-pig named Wimpy. They were most likely purchased, since I didn't learn what a pound or shelter was until my later teens. Years later, my aunt adopted a miniature pincher who we named Tuqui. Her cousin's dog had had puppies. Before Tuqui, there was Laika, the reason I loved going to visit my half-sister (apart from the pool in the backyard!). Laika, a pit bull purchased from a breeder, towered over my toddler-self and showered me with affection during each visit.

Reflecting on my growing up surrounded by nonhumans, I can now see how very early-on, I was subconsciously taught that, while some animals were for the home (purchased like things), others were to be *used* for various other purposes, beyond companionship. After three and a half decades, I can clearly track how that played into a deep-seeded acceptance of a "norm" that I didn't question until my mid-twenties. As a child, I loved all of my companion animals deeply, while not thinking twice about the ways in which I had unques-tionably drawn a line –between myself and "them," as well as between nonhumans themselves. There were instances in which I felt uncomfortable and knew something was wrong; but my mind would shrug and say, "That's just the way it is," and the world kept turning.

Poor Tuqui, my childhood dog, was a victim of "pure breed" modifications. In the 80s, it was commonplace to send these dogs to the vet to get their ears and tails cut off and molded in the particular style of the dog's breed as puppies. He happened to come home one day with bandaged ears and tail. He'd weep if anything touched them. Then there were the fighting roosters kept in tiny wire cages behind my mom's sister's home-- forced participants in a cultural tradition on the island: *pelea de gallos* (cockfighting).

I remember once being excited to go out on a small metal boat, *una yola*; under clear blue skies swaying over tropical waters, I watched my father wait for his victims to bite. The unlucky ones were placed in a closed cooler, slowly suffocating until their last breath. This was probably the first time I saw Caribbean reef fish, and I remember thinking how beautiful and unique they all were. My stepmother would later scrape the magical colors reflected off of the scales clean-off for dinner. I didn't eat that evening.

Thinking back to third grade, I can remember the color-dyed baby chicks that we received as gifts at school, just before Easter break. Because of their in-ability to produce eggs, these chicks were unwanted by the egg industry. Unfortunately, my oldest cousin, while in anger, took a wrong step and killed the defenseless chick while we were at my grandma's for Easter Sunday. She was jealous that she had not received a chick from her own school. I was inconsolable, but my grandmother assured me that nonhumans did not feel like us.

They were akin to robots – unaware of life or death – she claimed.

Yet other living beings close to me were clearly capable of being hurt and communicated in their own ways with me. I remember being confused by her words, which went against my real-life experiences and understanding of the world at that time.

That's just it: This perception that nonhumans did not feel pain, or anything at all, and thus didn't matter, was a "truth" that I simply accepted as a child. As children grow up, however, they start to make sense of the world on their own terms. At the same time, society moves on, and this means that many practices from the 80s, 90s, and 00s are illegal, perceived as cruel, or looked down on-- when committed against those who are deemed companion animals or by the hands of an individual, at least, since nonhumans used for food (pigs, chickens, cows, turkeys...), entertainment (horse races, cock fighting), clothing (fur and leather), etc. are still often ignored, and their abuse and slaughter accepted. Why?

I've now been vegan for over a decade and have only just begun to understand the answers to that question. My grandmother's reassurance that nonhumans were akin to *things* simply didn't make sense, yet I continued eating them and supporting industries that exploited and abused them. It's easy to go with traditions and the accepted social norms when we otherize and see those newly-created "others" as "less than." Depersonifying other living beings that experience life differently, communicate differently, and look so differently from us doesn't take very much when we set "human" as the superior way to exist in a world made up of thousands of different beings, each with their own experiences and abilities specific to them.

As I turned 25, the veiled that had convinced me that I was superior to all nonhumans and allowed me to ignore the suffering and individuality of other animals that I had recognized as a child was suddenly ripped from my eyes. I realized what my choices were supporting, and they just did not align with who I thought I was— someone who cared about *all* living beings and *all* marginalized communities. From then on, I continued to grow in my search for justice, and then it hit me...

I finally recognized, in my thirties, that I wasn't only taught to otherize and devalue nonhumans. History had taught me, since birth and through the same otherization accepted without question, that some groups of humans were less deserving, less valuable... simply, "less than." The worst part was realizing that nonhuman animals were a tool in order to justify this within our own communities, and that they are tools *still* employed against marginalized communities.

These personal realizations intermingled with the interconnections I came to learn about my own history outside of what we were taught in school:

Puerto Ricans have had a colonized identity for over 500 years, ever since our native people, *Tainos*, were assaulted, the male population "decimated" (Vilar 2013), and the women forced to mix with the white European colonizers, who then brought our African ancestors primarily as slaves to our island for forced labor. This is who we are: we are a people made up of a mixed ancestry. We—most Puerto Ricans— are tri-racial: Indigenous Caribbean (Taino), Western African, and European (Gravel et al. 2013).

Indigenous people and African slaves were not seen as people. Both groups of people were enslaved. They were merely seen by white Europeans as tools to use for profit. They were "otherized" and seen as exploitable—*things* to be used. Columbus himself is quoted as saying about the Tainos that, "They will give all that they do possess for anything that is given to them, exchanging things even for bits of broken crockery...They do not carry arms or know them...They should be good servants" (Poole 2011).

Servants. More accurately, forced slave laborers.

This included forcing Taino womxn and children into sex slavery— sold to the Spaniards (Thacher et al. 1903).

Once the Native people were killed off and mixed, Puerto Rico's colonized history moved on to include the use of African slaves, as well as free Africans (from non-colonies), in forced labor, as soldiers, and in repro-duction. African slavery continued in Puerto Rico, as the island became the largest producer and exporter of agriculturally-important crops, such as sugar, coffee, and tobacco (Minority Rights Group 2018). Those who lived on the island would now also include descendants of colonialism: a tri-racial population; the Puerto Rican of "today."

The Spanish eventually forced a clear, legal, and named racial caste system upon the island: white (including those who were mixed, but considered white), Indigenous, "Mestizos" (white mixed with Indigenous), Free People of Color, and Slaves. Economic status was determined by racial caste. Free People of Color experienced many of the same oppressions and restrictions as slaves, as they were considered part of the "contaminated" castes opposite whites and were encouraged to work towards whiteness in order to gain privileges (Kinsbruner 1996).

The site MinorityRights.Org explains that a large population of enslaved Africans, free People of Color, and "mixed" descendants meant that,

> *In order to limit the possibility of a rebellion or local independence the Spanish government imposed draconian racist laws, such as 'El Bando contra La Raza Africana', to control the behavior of all Puerto Ricans of African origin whether slave or free.*

> *With European settlers having official sanction, instances of cruelty towards the African workforce were routine. This helped to establish relationships in the society such as the low regard for African ancestry and African culture in general including devaluing dark skin colour and attendant hair texture.*

The "one-drop rule," put into effect once the U.S. became our colonizer (1898), declared that even a single African ancestor would result in a person being designated as Black. This pushed supremacist hierarchies into us even more. A common saying heard while I was growing up, *Hay que trabajar como negro para vivir como blanco,* exemplified the dynamic that we internalized without even realizing it: to live as a white person, we must work like a Black person in a white supremacist society dependent on racial casteism, where our non-white and non-light-skinned members get the least of everything in exchange for the hardest life and the most work.

Many Puerto Ricans assimilated and even suppressed their Black roots for survival once they were given U.S. citizenship. Afro-Boricuas were automatically considered Black in a time when African Americans (forcibly brought as slaves directly to the mainland) were openly discriminated against and segregated. However, just like in modern times, those with lighter skin privileges were able to claim they were white or mixed race and thus faced less discrimination.

If we are honest with ourselves and look within our communities, we can see that colonialism by Europeans (i.e. Spain) and later, the United States, gave root to the expansion of *colorism* (a form of prejudice based on believing that lighter skin is better) and *anti-blackness* (implicitly perceiving Black as "less than"). During colonialism, people of color were forced into a racial hierarchy with whiteness at the top. This same supremacist hierarchy *still* denies Black and Brown people their personhood and assigns values to our lives.

Devaluing the lives of other living beings— as was done to Indigenous, Africans, and mixed descendants— was possible through their "otherization," which is a tactic that separates a group or community by focusing on their differences and thereby, depersonifying them with the purpose of making them "less than" to the accepted way to be. In the case of Borikén, the Spanish otherized the Tainos, the African slaves, and their descendants in order to hold power over them, use them, enslave them, mistreat them, and justify their suffering and even their death. One tactic used to accomplish this was *animalization*: the purposeful denigration of marginalized groups to the level of nonhuman animals.

Have you ever stopped to ask yourself why nonhuman animals are considered less than humans, despite us all being biologically classified as members of the animal species; or why being called an animal is one of the biggest insults we humans can encounter?

Common thoughts may be:

"They look different from us".

"They don't speak like us".

"They are not as intelligent as us."

"They are less than us."

"They are things to be used by us."

Or like my grandmother had insisted, "They don't feel like us or have any awareness."

By whose standards, and why? These statements were certainly not true of my companion animals growing up. Despite science having repeatedly demonstrated that nonhuman animals have their own communities, practices, abilities, and even *language* unique to them and unrelated to human animals, we uphold a human supremacy-based hierarchy that otherizes them for their differences. These differences have been exploited through speciesism (humans above nonhumans) in order to enslave them, exploit them, and commodify them in horrific ways, as well as ultimately slaughter them and consume them by the billions without a thought– when we don't even need to because humans are biologically omnivores who can thrive on plant-based diets.

Conveniently, white supremacy routinely uses the otherization of nonhuman animals against People of

Color in a way that we have internalized racialized speciesism in which animalization, rooted in speciesism, upholds a hierarchy where white is at the top and People of Color are below *them*, but *just above* nonhuman animals. We are automatically born into a society that upholds whiteness, and we have learned, accepted, and co-opted the tools of otherization that uphold our place within a supremacist pyramid by exerting the same depersonifying mentality over other living beings.

In an article titled *Racialized Speciesism* (Feliz 2018), I discussed that,

> *In their book, Aph and Syl Ko explained that the classification system of human vs. animal is an idea founded on white male rationale. The authors argued that we must finally oppose the idea that human and animals are opposite - that nonhuman animals are also individuals on their own instead of a lump sum group that we see collectively as "them". Doing so would mean to begin to break the cycle of oppression that is kept in place through a system still purported by white supremacy.*

In the same article, I further explained that,

> *The mere idea that we, People of Color, are on the same level of nonhumans creates automatic defensiveness upheld by very real and ongoing systemic oppression because of what it has meant and what it still means today since racism, xenophobia, colorism, anti-blackness, etc. are still ongoing and very much part of our*

experience.

Bestia, burro, animal, cochino, cerdo, puerco, becerro, perro, gallina, rata, etc. are all Spanish words routinely used in Puerto Rico as insults against those we deem as "less than." They are all words that describe and come from nonhumans, or the actual names of nonhumans themselves. The same words were used to animalize and oppress our own throughout history. I'm sure I don't have to list examples of how our own communities have been compared to "lesser animals." If we look through our history and the history of other communities, we can see that animalization is often invoked when those in power intend on justifying their abuse over marginalized people. African slaves, Jewish people, and the Tutsis of Rwanda are but a few examples of human communities depersonified through the otherization of nonhuman animals. We're even seeing this happen right now, at this very point in history, being used to devalue the lives of Latinx and Black refugees and immigrants looking for help and safety from the United States.

In essence, we've been duped through white supremacy and racialized speciesism into helping to keep our own system of oppression going. We've internalized the idea that others can be "less than" because of their differences, and we unconsciously uphold the tools of our oppressors and invoke them ourselves against those we've been told we are like yet strive to be better than – nonhuman animals.

So, what would happen if we rejected animalization—otherization through nonhumans— and took the power away from it by acknowledging that our oppressions are interconnected? What would happen if we refused to follow the same tactics that have followed us and led us to this mess of a society? Centuries of history that have led up to this moment in time must be addressed. To understand the interconnections of our oppression and to fight against it is to decenter whiteness and fight back against white supremacy.

Apart from the ethics of standing up against the abuse and needless death of living beings, I ask that you consider, as a step towards understanding the inter-connections between our oppressions, how anima-lization has been used as a tool against your own co-mmunity and other communities of color.

I've lived outside of Borikén now for many years, but I feel that my understanding of where I came from, how, and what my role should be was aided by being exposed to other communities and truly taking the time to listen to their struggles. My advocacy is devoted to **consistent anti-oppression** across social justice movements committed towards the liberation of both humans and nonhumans. Why? Because in my mind, I must consistently fight against *all* oppression, including anti-blackness, and that fight must also include nonhuman animals.

Thus, at 36, what it means for me to be vegan has evolved from a fight for some into a fight for us all. It's a fight that decenters whiteness by rejecting the tools that it has used to oppress my people since they landed on the shores of Borikén over five centuries ago.

Cited Works

Feliz, Julia (2018). Racialized Speciesism? *Medium.com*: https://medium.com/@jd.feliz/racialized-speciesism-991eb3653ba0

Gravel S., Zakharia F., Moreno-Estrada A, Byrnes JK, Muzzio M, Rodriguez-Flores JL, et al. (2013). Reconstructing Native American Migrations from Whole-Genome and Whole-Exome Data. *PLoS Genet*. 9(12).

Kinsbruner, Jay (1996). *Not of Pure Blood: The Free People of Color and Racial Prejudice in Nineteenth-Century Puerto Rico*, Duke University Press Books: 19-21.

MinorityReport.Org (2018) *Afro-Puerto Ricans*: http://minorityrights.org/minorities/afro-puerto-ricans

Poole, Robert M. (2011). What Became of the Taino? *Smithsonian.com*: https://www.smithsonianmag.com /travel/what-became-of-the-taino73824867

Thacher, John B (1903). Christopher Columbus: his life, his work, his remains as revealed by original printed and manuscript records, together with an essay on Peter Martyr of Anghera and Bartolomé de las Casas, the first historians of America. *G.P. Putnam's Sons*: 426-427.

Vilar, Miguel (2014). Genographic Project DNA Results Reveal Details of Puerto Rican History. *Changing Planet in National Geographic Blog:* https://blog.national geographic.org/2014/07/25/genographic-project-dna-results-reveals-details-of-puerto-rican-history

Identity and Interconnections from a Wiradjuri First Nations Woman

By Carolyn Ienna

I am a Wiradjuri first nations woman. The Wiradjuri are the largest group of First Nations people, residing on the biggest land mass on the continent that white people call "Australia." Although I live on Gadigal land, we have no one name for the continent.

While I am a Wiradjuri from my mother's side, I am also Sicilian from my Father's side of the family and have strong ties with that. My father's family migrated to this country two generations back. I am a dancer, performer, spoken word/rapper, artist, costume maker, and more. I am pretty nerdy, too; and I am vegan, which has become a large part of my identity, as have all of my other passions.

I originally went vegan for my health, and it did help me. However, I became chronically ill and nearly died that year— back in 1985. Eventually, I realized that all of the nonhuman animals that I had seen tortured and killed in front of me were really the reasons why veganism made sense to me. I remember going to factory farms as a child, and there's nothing any video can show that compares to the horrors I saw and still have in my memories. The smell of those places haunts me, and I just want to liberate them all. At the time I went vegan, I didn't communicate any of this for a long time because of the harassment I received when I first lived as a vegetarian. However, times are different now. As time passed, I saw the interconnections between veganism and sexism, racism, and even colorism; so, my reasons for being vegan are now because of both nonhuman and human liberation.

I became vegan before my mum told me who we were. Hiding someone's first nations identity is very common on this continent. My family, as far as I know, were not stolen or from the "stolen generation," in which Aboriginal children were stolen and placed with white families in order to force assimilation on them. For my mother and her family, it was just a matter of survival to pretend to not be Aboriginal so they could get a job, get partners, and simply live in peace and have opportunities denied to those who did not hide. For those that were separated, it takes a long time, if it is to happen at all, to reconnect, because the government hid our people's records for a long time.

Since learning who I am and where I come from, I have learned about my people and our views of the world. For example, Wiradjuri elders teach the respect all life through song lines. We don't have written language, so these songs tell stories that often remind us that humans never have dominion over any other being. Some of our stories speak about other animals, like the serpent, as creators. Some stories speak of nonhumans as our ancestors. Each clan will have its own stories, though. Nature is usually our mother, and those who are initiated may even be given names from non-human animals. Totems are spiritual symbols from nature and part of our identity and culture, and interestingly, if a clan, family, or even an individual has a "totem" animal, then you cannot kill or eat that specific animal. Sadly, many of our native animals have gone extinct since the onset of the colonization of our continent.

I find that, in connection to my culture, veganism to me is essential, as nonhumans are a marginalized community, like my Wiradjuri people still are. Non-humans are otherized so that their exploitation and abuse can be justified. It's easier to disregard the lives of "the other," as was done to Aboriginal people. We were once even classified as part of the fauna by white settlers. In addition, nonhumans are stolen from their imprisoned mothers for the creation of things like dairy, just as we were and still are. It was done to us under the "stolen generation," which most people think has come and gone, but the white government is taking our children at a higher rate now than ever before in history (Wahlquist 2018). These children are still placed in the care of non-Aboriginals— never with family or Aboriginal-led organizations. Aboriginal people also have the highest incarceration rate in the world (Anthony 2017). This reminds me of the imprisonment of the millions of nonhumans forced into the factory farming system every year. Systemically, we die twenty years younger than the rest of the population even though there is a scheme called "Close the Gap" that the government imple-mented over a decade ago, which was aimed at raising the health and life expectancy of Aboriginal people. These are just a few ways in which Aboriginal people are still routinely oppressed, of many, including work discrimination, classism, police brutality without accountability, etc.

The wildlife we remember in our stories are either now extinct and have been forced to leave their homes, much like our people have also been forced to leave our lands. The white government continues to close down remote aboriginal communities by cutting off funding, which meant cutting off water and other resources (Madden 2015). This so that mining companies can grab traditional homelands for their own profit (Gregoire 2015). Animal agriculture used for cattle grazing is also another means through which our land has been stolen and exploited (ACLUMP 2018). Factory farming, brought in with colonialism, is a direct way in which our own rights have been violated. Thus, most Aboriginal people that I meet do not live a traditional life.

From the beginning of our colonization, the reality is that our oppression has always been interconnected with the oppression of nonhuman animals through our otherization. Would it not make sense for those of us who have the ability to do so to rise up and fight back against the white government by ensuring that we disconnect from nonhuman animal oppression and exploitation? To do so would be to fight against the same otherization that gave them power to steal from us— all of us. To do so would be to connect with our storylines, which speak of our peaceful relations with other animals. We know of the spirits that are within all beings and that they communicate with us. They tell us about the weather, when to build shelter, when a fruit is ripe, and when danger is coming. What would they tell us about our own hand in their oppression, and our own?

Cited Works

ACLUMP (2018). *Land Use in Australia – At a Glance.* Australian Collaborative Land Use Mapping Programme. Accessed October 14, 2018: http://www.agriculture. gov.au/abares/aclump/Documents/Land_use_in_Austral ia_at_a_glance_2006.pdf

Anthony, T. (2017). Fact Check Q&A: are Indigenous Australians the most incarcerated people on Earth? *TheConversation.com*: https://theconversation .com/factcheck-qanda-are-indigenous-australians-the-most-incarcerated-people-on-earth-78528

Gregoire, P. (2015). Are Mining Interests Behind Western Australian Remote Aboriginal Community Closures? *VICE News*: https://www.vice.com/en_us/article/exqp3k/are-mining-interests-behind-western-australian-remote-aboriginal-community-closures

Madden, C. (2015) Forced Closures of Aboriginal Communities in Australia Continue. *Cultural Survival News:* https://www.culturalsurvival.org/news/forced-closures-aboriginal-communities-australia-continue

Wahlquist, C. (2018). Indigenous children in care doubled since stolen generations apology. *The Guardian:* https://www.theguardian.com/australia-news/2018/jan/25/indigenous-children-in-care-doubled-since-stolen-generations-apology

The Shift from Hierarchy to Interconnection: My Path to Veganism

By Towani Duchscher

My path to veganism started with Eric Garner.

His murder was not new. It has been going on since African people were kidnapped and enslaved in North America; but now, for me, for us, in this time, this oppression was presented to the public, on television, for everyone to see. As a society, we watched Eric Garner beg for his life (New York Daily News 2015). We watched his last breath. I had never seen a person killed. I cannot un-see that. Watching six police officers press his life out on the sidewalk, the way they might put out a cigarette with the bottom of their heel, was a physical representation of the oppression of the African-American people. The word *oppression* comes from Latin *oppressionem,* meaning "a pressing down" (Oppression n.d.). The public watched the act of oppression and its result: the pressing out of a man's life onto the dirty sidewalk. We watched it over and over and over again. I will never forget that. Nor should I. That video will haunt me forever.

What added additional pain was the implicit and explicit acceptance that followed his murder. There were no consequences for the police officers. The general society accepted this act. The general society accepted that a man could be killed on the street, in broad daylight, by the police, and his death could be recorded and played for entertainment on the news. It is one thing to dismiss the oppression that you may not see or experience; but, when it is presented to you, explicitly, there is no excuse. I struggled to understand how the majority of people could even continue their days after watching someone die. Then I realized that most people were able to continue their days because they did not just watch "someone" die; they watched a *black* man die, and that was, apparently, different. This helped me to understand that underlying and supporting all forms of oppression is a complex history of educating people to first fragment ourselves into groups and then place those fragmented pieces into a hierarchy (Sensoy & DiAngelo 2012; Stanton n.d.). This hierarchy of fragmentation allows people to distance themselves from others and place diminishing levels of value on the lives we deem to be beneath us. I knew then that my PhD research needed to examine the ways that schools teach students to believe in and perpetuate this fragmentation and hierarchy.

At that time, I was a meat eater. I always felt that eating meat was part of my experience of my culture. I am mixed race. My father was a black man from Trinidad and my mother a white woman of British decent. My parents were divorced, and I lived with my mother in a small, mostly Caucasian town. My experience of my Caribbean culture and identity was limited. Much of my connection to my Caribbean culture revolved around the food, and that food was mostly centered around meat. Eating meat was part of how I identified as Caribbean, but I had not thought about the consequences of my food choices.

Shortly after watching Eric Garner die, a classmate in one of the PhD courses I was taking asked our class to watch the movie *Earthlings* (Monson et al. 2010). I did not know what *Earthlings* was about; I did not know that I was about to be witness to the multitude of ways that humans use, abuse, and discard animal life. I was not prepared to watch that much death and suffering. I had to watch it in pieces. I finished each chunk dissolved in tears. It was too much. However, I felt that was an appropriate response to watching a being die. I was watching the life forced out of a living being, over and over and over again. I will never forget that. Nor should I.

Surprisingly, I kept eating meat for a few more months; but I could not un-see those images, those deaths. The images continued to challenge me until I could no longer stand my own hypocrisy. How could I say that I believed in equality and wanted to fight against fragmentation and hierarchy, when I had placed myself into a hierarchy with nonhuman animals? I had to confront the fact that my actions were not aligned with my beliefs. I had to confront the fact that the arguments for eating meat were many of the same arguments used to support the slavery of my ancestors (Caplan 2015). I had to confront the fact that, if I wanted to fight for freedom from oppression for myself and my children— and Eric Garner's children, too— I must fight for freedom for *all* living beings.

So, my family and I stopped eating meat and dairy and started seeing ourselves as interconnected with the world. I started understanding my Caribbean culture and identity as something that goes deeper than meat. I started seeing a connection between all animals, human and nonhuman. My world view shifted from a hierarchy to an interconnected web.

For me, the path to veganism started with confronting the beliefs that were supporting my actions and realigning myself with new beliefs. Fragmentation and hierarchy are interwoven so deeply in many of our beliefs that we often cease to see this connection. This belief system is weighing us down, pressing down upon us, oppressing us as living beings. It's too much. We "can't breathe" (New York Daily News 2015).

Cited Works

Caplan, G. (2015). How do we justify the horrible things we've done? *The Globe and Mail*. Retrieved from https://www.theglobeandmail.com/news/politics/how-do-we-justify-the-horrible-things-weve-done/article25184138/

Monson, S., White, P., Moby, M.Q., Phoenix, J., Nation Earth Organization., & Earthlings.com (Firm). (2010). *Earthlings*. Burbank, CA: Earthlings.com.

New York Daily News (2015). *Eric Garner video-Unedited version*: https://www.youtube.com/watch?v=JpGxagKOkv8

Oppression. (n.d.) In *Online Etymology Dictionary*: http://www.etymonline.com

Sensoy, O., & DiAngelo, R. (2012). *Is everyone really equal? An introduction to key concepts in social justice education.* New York, NY: Teachers College Press.

Stanton, G.H. (n.d.). The ten stages of genocide. *Genocide Watch*: http://www.genocidewatch.org /genocide/tenstagesofgenocide.html

The Intersection of Casteism and Speciesism: Interconnections from a Dalit

By Prateek Gautam

Since it's been more than 70 years since India's independence— along with things like Article 17 of our constitution, which abolished untouchability, and laws like the Scheduled Castes and Tribes (Prevention of Atrocities) Act of 1989, which gave legal protections to marginalized castes— one may conclude that untouchability and the caste system are in the past. The reality, however, is far from that. People's views on untouchability and the caste system have not truly evolved, despite changes in legislation.

You might think that I am exaggerating but pick up today's newspaper and head to the matrimonial section, or visit any matrimonial site, and you will see clear examples of casteism in place. Stalin K's 2007 documentary titled "India Untouched: Stories of a People Apart" shows how, even in recent times, high-class priests (I should say "elite class" Hindu priests), like Batuprasad Sharma Shashtri, strongly believe in and practice these customs, and have even specified a willingness to risk time in jail for them:

> *Let me introduce myself. My name is Batu-prasad Sharma Shashtri, I am the disciple of Swami Kripatriji Maharaj. I am the chief priest of The Tulsi Manas Temple (one of the five most important temples in Varanasi). I am also the General Secretary of the Scholars' association in*

Varanasi. As a believer of the Shastras (Holy Scriptures), I am an alt right and fundamentalist Hindu Brahmin and I believe in caste system and untouchability.

Later in the documentary, Batuprasad continued,

I've been arrested several times under anti-untouchability act when chamars (Dalits) would enter the Vishwanath Temple, we, the big scholars, would say that they would be sinning if they enter the temple, so we would kick them out! And I am not afraid to do that again.

In justifying his point of view, Batuprasad added,

God created Shudras, Kshatriyas, Brahmins and the entire universe. He has prescribed specific jobs for everyone. Why did you get the birth as a Shudra? Why did you get the birth of a woman? Why do you have black skin or white skin? All these are the results of the karma of our several births. A Dalit doesn't have the right to education; he cannot understand what's written in Vedas or Shashtras or other rights, which are only meant for other castes. Our Veda and Shastra are orders. Obey it –you have no right to judge it. It is written in our Shashtras that only animals follow intelligence, humans follow Shashtras.

Thus, according to his views, people that do not follow Vedas and their principles are "dumb," like nonhuman animals and "inferior," while those who follow Vedas are superior to all animals and humans. In the mind of Batuprasad, an elite priest for the upper caste, lower castes are akin to other animals and upper castes are above all in a hierarchical caste system.

One of the elements that has fueled and powered the caste system in modern times, apart from intra-caste marriages and strict rules, is the enslavement of nonhuman animals and the further division of them— also based on caste. The use of animals for various purposes— including food, clothing, entertainment, labor, and other forms of exploitation— defines how pure and high a caste is. Purity, in India, based on nonhuman animal casteism, is used as a reference to discriminate between different castes and uphold supremacist hierarchies. Human rights activists use a specific term known as "Brahmanism mentality" to name this type of hierarchical discrimination based on purity. However, the term is limited to humans only and does not reflect how nonhuman animals form part of upholding casteism. In truth, the mainstream public has failed to recognize the fact that oppression based on caste, race, or religion is rooted in the same justifications and interconnections as the oppression based on species.

Casteist speciesism conceptualizes the addition of nonhuman oppression as a driving force that allows casteism to continue unchecked. Under this type of speciesism, nonhumans are given a value according to caste: Cows are considered holy and sacred while pigs are impure, filthy, and dirty and should not be allowed anywhere near a temple or near higher-caste people. Horses are the pride and property limited to Kshatriyas only, while Dalits and Shudras are forbidden to ride horses and camels— even today, in parts of Rajasthan and Gujrat. Milk and milk products are considered pure and holy and represented as Lord Krishna's or Shiva's favorite food, whereas an animal's flesh is considered as "Chandals" (devil's) food and associated with the "lower" castes.

Adding to the interconnections, we find that, while some nonhuman animals have been deemed sacred, the pain, cries, and torture of others is accepted and ignored. Other animals are entirely dependent on humans and their customs in a caste-based society that continues to thrive in India. People who drink milk are considered pure, while people who consume cows' and pigs' flesh are considered dirty. Ever heard how Babas, yogis, Shashtris and Veda philosophers insist on how important ghee is? Or the insistence on the "holy" importance of milk? What about the religious application of honey? Milk, ghee, curd, honey, and butter are described as some of the purest offerings to God from humans. These same "godmen" use tiger skins because they are considered sacred. Similarly, bull horns are used as good luck charms, and some animals are even sacrificed to "rid" oneself of evil. For many, riding a mare at one's marriage is a caste tradition under casteism, as riding or owning a horse is allowed to only some upper caste people like the Rajputs, Thakurs, etc. Riding a horse through the streets is a status symbol and display of caste dominance, which is why many still continue to do so, while other upper caste groups take part in things like bullfights to show how strong a male from a caste is.

Even choosing what part of the animals should be used for what purpose reflects caste. Milk for Brahmins, farming for Vaishyas, hides and leather for Kshatriyas, and finally, flesh and other "waste parts" for Shudras. Plant-based foods and foods based on animal by-products, such as ghee, curd, and milk, are forbidden for the lower castes. It was considered a sin for a Dalit to own any of these, and, in order to survive, they turned to "unholy" and "impure" sources of food. Historically, Dalits were basically denied their own lands and hence were unable to farm on their own.

After India's independence, many things did change; for example, many Dalits are now given land and further support from the government. However, the mindset of upper-caste people remains somewhat the same. After generations upon generations in which people were forced to eat certain foods or live in certain ways, it becomes cemented as their lifestyle. Thus, many Dalits, even today, are dependent on sources of animal foods forced upon them by the upper castes.

Often, we hear people say that they treat the other animals in their life "like they are family members." However, when we truly look at the relationship between humans and other animals, this is an inaccurate perception of the reality. These animals are beneficial assets– property. When a cow or buffalo is healthful and well, they are used for the milk they produce, which is intended for their calves. The calves, however, are committed to a life of farming, or impregnated again for their own milk. This system is kept in place to satisfy the request of Brahmins to buy and consume the "purest" form of what is animal exploitation. These "pure" milk products are also made as offerings in temples and also keep the cycle of hierarchy and inequality running.

Today, even after the many steps taken by government and law enforcements to curb casteism, upper castes still consider it a sin if a Dalit owns or touches whatever they aren't supposed to own or touch. This means that even employment is tied to nonhuman-dependent caste hierarchies. Countless numbers of cows, bulls, oxen, buffaloes, horses, chickens, pigs, donkeys and elephants die serving different purposes for different caste groups. When these animals become "useless," Dalits are expected to clean the "mess." Dalits are given the task of slaughtering them to sell their flesh and peel off their skins, wash, dry, and clean them for leather, which Vaishyas then purchase for very little money in order to mold the skins into leather shoes and musical instruments. These, by the way, are "end products" of a hierarchy-based chain that traditionally and according to Vedas only Brahmins are allowed to use. In essence, thousands-year-old traditions have not changed. Any factory that makes animal skin into a wearable leather is completely filled with Dalit workers, who are usually not even rewarded with permanent employment. In a documentary made by National Geographic titled "Inside an Indian Tannery," horrific working conditions of tannery workers are shown, and all of the workers we see belong to marginalized communities, including Dalits and lower-caste Muslims.

We find more examples of inequality in jobs like manual scavenging, which is a large and mostly ignored problem in India. The majority of waste management in

India is done manually and is most ignored because it involves only Dalits and "untouchables." Recently, a protest happened at Jantar Manter to end manual scavenging, which has killed more than 1,000 sanitation workers over the past year– eleven in the week before the protest itself. All of them were Dalits. The event was covered by Jayashree Bajoria of The Wire news agency. She interviewed one of the protest attendees, named Bablu, who explained:

> We don't get any other job, no matter where we go. I have tried. I know this is discrimination, but what can I do? I was thrilled when I secured a job interview in a hotel because I wanted to train as a waiter. But as soon as the manager heard my caste, I was hired instead to clean toilets. Others with a similar education, who were not Dalit, got the waiter jobs.

Bablu explained that soon after, he quit the hotel job and was compelled to take manual scavenging as a job for his survival. Bablu's struggle exemplifies how, even today, caste-based discrimination exists just like it always has.

Adding to this, we find that workers from other departments, such as the railway department, have openly disclosed that, for example, in railways, only Dalits are hired specifically to clean things like railways tracks and to pick-up and dispose of deceased human and nonhuman animal bodies. During an interview for the "India Untouched" documentary, one of the workers explained:

> *I belong to the dom (Dalit) caste. My whole neighborhood works for the railways on contract basis. We dispose of all dead bodies found on the railway tracks. A speeding train cuts the body into many pieces. So, we pick up those pieces from here and from there and put the body back together, photos are taken and then it is sent for post mortem.* Another worker added that, *we carry rotten bodies on our shoulders, even after ten days, stinking smells doesn't go. We work as daily wage or on contract but are never directly hired by the railways.*

Whenever a "holy cow" dies, Dalits are charged with picking up the remains of the body and burying it. Somehow, these supposedly holy animals that are claimed to be thought of as family become "untouchable" after their death. Dalits are forced to do some of the dirtiest work when it comes to nonhuman animals, and it benefits only the oppressors –not the victims of the oppressive system. Dalits and nonhuman animals are *both* unwilling victims.

Once we draw the lines across the relationships that our society has forced between different castes and nonhumans, we can clearly see that "Brahminism ideology," upheld through *casteist speciesism*, success-fully keeps the caste system intact though a dependency on the oppression and exploitation of nonhuman animals. In essence, apart from helping the nonhuman animal liberation movement gain much pace and strength, taking nonhuman animals out of the equation by embracing vegan ethics and lifestyle would hurt the caste system and destabilize its whole structure. Adopting a vegan stance would be a way to remove hierarchies that distinguish between pure and impure, between both humans and nonhumans. Therefore, rejecting our own speciesist hierarchy by eliminating nonhumans from the equation would disallow the use of "food politics," which, as we've seen, keeps the human caste system firmly in place.

Rejecting Speciesism and Casteism: A Hindu Perspective

By Rama Ganesan

The following statement is specifically meant for nonvegan people of color from my own background and upbringing— people from India who are Hindu and have inherited the hierarchical thought structures regarding castes.

Caste structures are described in some of our ancient Hindu scriptures. They have been introduced into the more general culture and have found their way into the practices of other religions in India, such as Islam and Christianity. However, these structures exist most clearly within the Hindu religion in the present day. Here, I want to discuss casteism and how it relates to speciesism. To live in a world that is free of oppression, we have to address both structures of domination.

As Hindus, we assign a unique role to cows in our society. As animals that produce milk, we revere them as "mother." We consider that it is the purpose of the cow to produce milk for us, rather than their own babies, just as we might consider oxen to be animals that are intended to pull carts. Neither of these animals agreed to adopt these roles for us; we have forced them into them. Seeing the cow as our mother might make us feel that we are entitled to her milk. In reality, cows did not consent to "give" us milk, or to be our mothers. Cows have their own calves, and those are the animals they want to nurture.

We do not need cow's milk to survive or to be healthy. We are holding on to the mistaken notion that children especially need cow's milk. Cow's milk is not the right food for humans at any stage of our lives. It is one of the most common allergens among children. When my son was small, my elder relatives were shocked that he didn't drink milk. That boy, with his strange allergies and food preferences, was a forerunner to the current generation of allergy-stricken children. He had his own views on what he would eat, and he kept away from foods that bothered him. However, even if were not for allergies and preferences, it became clear to me that there is no reason for us to be drinking the milk of another species.

We pride ourselves on our purity from our meatless diets, yet we do not recognize how milk is the same as meat, in a liquid form. Perhaps its whiteness has something to do with its perceived purity. Of course, we do not kill the cow to get the milk, and, because of this, we can ease our conscience and feel superior to those who eat meat. In reality, we deprive calves of their mothers' milk, tie them up in temples and let them die, saying it the gods' will. The difference between flesh and milk is actually miniscule.

Social hierarchy and classification by societal function were a part of my upbringing. This includes both speciesism and casteism. Some animals have certain roles to play, and we use them for these purposes. Similarly, some humans have certain roles to play, and we use them for those purposes. As species membership is inherited, so is caste inherited. Our role in life is predetermined by our lineage. Some of us are of the highest caste– we are the revered priests and teachers, the upper echelon of privilege. Then the other high castes are tasked with being the rulers, merchants, and peasants. Finally, we reach those who are below caste altogether: the people from the villages, forest-dwellers, and street people who are tasked with the most menial and degrading work.

I remember, as a child, watching a cow being milked, and then watching her calf trying to get milk. I have been pulled in carts by bulls and oxen. In the same way, I remember seeing humans, adults and children, walk the streets and unpaved roads wearing next to nothing in the hot sun. I was taught that this is the way it is supposed to be. We inherit our station in life, whether it is our species or our caste. We get what we deserve, and there is no further need to question it. Yes, some people are destitute, naked, disfigured, objects of violence; I am supposed to disregard them.

Some of what I learned about caste go way back into very early childhood and I do not remember them specifically. But the following are some recollections.

I do remember my elder relative, who was around to see India's fight for freedom from the British Empire. I remember her qualifying and correcting my view of Gandhi, saying that Mahatma Gandhi was of a different caste from us. She specifically used the word *Jati*, which refers to sub-caste divisions, but I know that this relative just meant, "not one of us." I sat on the kitchen floor on a hot afternoon, while the water was boiling, and the coffee was being made. I was six or seven, and I remember being confused and disappointed. The Father of our Nation is not of the same caste as I am; we are different, I realized. It didn't make sense because the Mahatma is someone we admire— not someone we denigrate for being a lower caste.

All throughout my early childhood, I knew that the people who worked as servants in my small house— doing laundry, washing dishes, mopping floors— were low-caste. A different man would pick up the garbage from our yard periodically. The garbage was thrown into a hole dug out in the Earth. It is the inherited occupation of certain castes to perform this job.

An older relative compared a lower-caste servant girl to me once, saying she looked better than I did. This relative at once teased and complimented the girl; but the implication was how topsy-turvy it was that a servant-caste girl should look better than an upper-caste girl like me: *Look how the lower castes have advanced!*

After my son's *upanayanam* (a coming-of-age cere- mony for upper-caste boys), the Brahmin clergy objected to eating lunch if in the visible presence of the lower- caste humans, and my relatives acquiesced to their wishes to send the lower-caste humans away— out of sight.

Speciesism and casteism are the similar in that they are both about assigning different values to individuals based on a category membership. These value systems do not really exist in reality; they are merely artificial hierarchies that humans have imposed on those around us. Of course, I want you to be vegan and to recognize that cows should not be exploited for their milk. However, this alone is not enough when our culture and, especially, those closest to us continue to hold on to casteist hierarchies in our minds and interactions.

If we are going to dismantle hierarchies and oppression, you cannot hold on to one while eschewing another. Veganism is but one step in ridding ourselves from our hand in oppression. We must extend justice, understanding, and respect beyond those we deem above us or on our same level. Once we choose to embrace veganism, our path towards equality must also extend to those who have been considered "lower" than us.

The West has the impression that India is populated by peaceful and animal-loving vegetarians. It is tempting to only share aspects of our culture that reflect well on us. However, India is casteist, and Indians being a vegetarian often has nothing to do with loving or respecting nonhuman animals; it is about establishing our own "purity" in contrast to others who are considered "polluted." It is our own Brahmanic authority over Hindu history and cultural representation to the West that has skewed what India and Hinduism really is. This has left everyone in the U.S. and beyond thinking that Hinduism is the religion of *Ahimsa,* and that *Ahimsa* is equivalent to veganism. I am able to acknowledge that this is a false representation, as we Brahmins have only exported a one-sided view of Hinduism to the West—

one that erases the voices of the lower castes.

Just as I seek out and willingly learn about the atrocities in non-human animal exploitation, I also choose to seek and learn about caste discrimination and caste violence in India and outside of it. This has allowed me to open my eyes to the insidious ways in which caste hierarchy is perpetuated, even when we move to other countries. One of the more insidious of these ways is endogamy: a practice in which our second-generation children are pressured to marry into the same caste (which was shown in a deceptively innocent manner in the movie, *Meet the Patels*). Even more blatant caste discrimination has been reported among Indian expatriates. A recent survey of castes in the United States among South Asians revealed discrimination in schools, colleges, workplaces, and religious institutions (Equality Labs 2018).

Oppression is interconnected, and we must work against all the oppression that we have been conditioned to accept without question– both towards nonhumans and lower castes. We must dismantle both casteism and speciesism collectively in India and among expatriate Indians. We will need to examine how our holidays, our daily practices, and even how our names perpetuate caste hierarchies. We need to listen to the voices of Dalits and other oppressed peoples. Only at that point will we be embraced into a larger humanity that has been "re-enchanted" (*Aphro-ism* by Aph and Syl Ko 2017). The journey seems daunting; however, there is freedom at the end, and that brings benefits for us all as a whole.

Cited Works

Equality Labs (2018). *Caste in the United States: A Survey of Caste Among South Asian Americans*. Equality Labs: http://www.equalitylabs.org/caste-survey-2018

Norris, J. and Messina, V. (2011). *Vegan for Life: Everything You Need to Know to Be Healthy and Fit on a Plant-Based Diet*. Da Capo Lifelong Books.

Breaking with Tradition, or Tradition Redefined?

By Cina Ebrahimi

Growing up in a semi-traditional Iranian family with a fair amount of religious leaning, I was taught from an early age that nonhuman animals, like human animals, had rights and were entitled to respect. At the same time, however, this same belief system held that it was acceptable for humans to use nonhuman animals (for food, clothing, etc.) just as long as certain protocols were met in regard to how they were raised and killed.

Despite this, for as long as I could remember, part of me always felt that consuming other animals was wrong. Maybe not intrinsically wrong, but at least circumstantially wrong (I was not living in such a place that required me to kill other animals in order to feed or clothe myself). I always knew that nonhumans felt pain, and, since most humans have an interest in *not* being in pain, the only logical conclusion, to me, was that nonhuman animals *also* have an interest in not feeling pain. So, why were we so comfortable with inflicting pain on nonhuman animals when we know that doing so causes them the same feeling we humans try so diligently to avoid?

Fast forward to the year 2004— the summer before I started high school. I was just getting into "activism" by attending anti-George Bush rallies and getting into hardcore punk bands like Black Flag and Minor Threat. One day, as I was sitting on the flatbed of a pick-up truck full of friends in the middle of the backwoods somewhere near North Bend, Washington, Brad— another guy from our crew— came towards our truck and asked to ride along with us, since there was no room left in the other vehicles in our convoy. I can't remember how it came up, but we started talking about vegetarianism. This is when Brad mentioned that he was actually a "vegan." I had heard that term prior to this point in time, but I had always just thought it was a synonym for vegetarian. After he had explained what veganism was, someone else had asked why he made the jump to that after being vegetarian. He simply responded that while his reason for vegetarianism was due to guilt with what happened to nonhuman animals, the guilt did not stop there. He explained that cows were literally sexually violated in order to produce milk. That was the first time I had ever heard of that. However, like most things that I heard that bothered me, I simply said to myself how terrible it was and went back to life as usual.

In the following years, as I had gotten more politically active (as far as I could, for a kid still in high school), I periodically toyed with the question of why so many people fighting for human rights seemed to outright ignore nonhuman animal rights, and, in some cases, even fought *against* the animal rights movement. I eventually realized that I wasn't doing anything to that end myself, so I was quick to disregard it for fear of being a hypocrite. After all, I conveniently forgot about it as I settled in front of a plate of buffalo wings; how could I judge anyone else for doing the same?

When I was a freshman in college, I finally decided to become a vegetarian (as in I didn't eat meat, but still ate dairy and eggs). The desire to fully live that decision waxed and waned over the years; in fact, there were times when I was still eating meat while telling people that I was a vegetarian. While being involved in several activist circles I met the occasional vegan or two, and I simply said I was interested (whatever that meant at the time) in animal rights.

The question of whether to consider nonhuman animals deserving of moral consideration grew more significant to me following 9/11.

The oppression of others was easy to forget when viewed through a vacuum; but, when I viewed the oppression of nonhuman animals in the same light as the oppression that I experienced as an Iranian-American in the aftermath of 9/11— such as being called a "terrorist," or being adversely treated because of how I looked— it became absolutely impossible to ignore. If I, as someone from a marginalized background, felt that my rights deserved to be considered, then what was my justification for continuing to eat and wear the bodies of nonhuman animals? My viewpoint wasn't exactly popular, though, as many others from similar backgrounds felt that the idea of nonhuman animals and their rights was a hindrance to the acceptance of their own humanity, or a distraction from their own fight for liberation.

I found myself going through an internal dialogue as it applied to my own community. Why would anyone think that being compared to animals is offensive? Why was it ok to mistreat animals in the first place? No one ever seemed to question that position; they just took it at face value. It was one thing (and, in fact, made sense) that privileged white males would view nonhuman animals as unequivocally deserving of oppression; after all, they've been responsible for so much other oppression. Why, though, would people who are aware of oppression be so ready to enact that same oppression on others, simply due to species membership? Were they really learning anything about their own oppression (and how to dismantle or not perpetuate it) if they enacted it on others?

These questions, which I have yet to find an answer to, had compelled me to forego as far as I could using things or engaging in practices that exploited nonhuman animals, and it was this that has kept me following a vegan lifestyle. Adopting a vegan "lifestyle," something that I had previously thought only pertained to food, included things such as clothing, personal care items, and even seemingly harmless activities such as attending zoos or horseback riding. While I did make this decision in terms of my food choices, I later began to learn of how certain non-food items, such as clothing and personal care items, were built on animal exploitation as well, which led me to make decisions in regards to those things. Whether it was testing ingredients using torturous methods on non-human animals or clothing that were made from skin torn off of their bodies, or forms of entertainment that were built on their kidnapping and imprisonment.

I finally made the switch to becoming a vegan (or, as some put it, an "animal person") in 2014, and I haven't looked back since. In going back to the traditions I was raised with and how they related to food, I could not reconcile my consumption of animal bodies with my cultural and religious values that dictate that good deeds done for animals are tantamount to good deeds done for humans, and, conversely, that bad deeds committed against animals are tantamount to bad deeds committed against humans. Yes, certain foods and practices of my Muslim faith did involve the consumption of nonhuman animals; but continuing in these practices were completely incongruent with the same values they taught regarding respect for the right of nonhuman animals. It became clear to me that following traditional cultural practices was in the understanding and application of those teachings, rather than the physical act of consuming their bodies. I didn't have to choose between the religious teaching I grew up with and my personal convictions, because those religious teachings were in line with concept of avoiding both the unnecessary suffering of any sentient creature and the environmental degradation of the earth, something animal exploitation is the number one cause of.

When people ask me how I can still stay true to my cultural integrity while living a vegan life, I simply say that there is no contradiction at all; in fact, to consume the bodies of nonhuman animals would put me at odds with my cultural integrity. Exploiting nonhumans when it's not necessary for my survival would necessarily mean to violate the rights of the nonhuman animals, whom I had been taught to respect.

Every so often, I get people asking me why I refuse to not consume non-humans, often by way of the notion that they were created for human use. But nothing could be further from the truth, the idea that humans are somehow separate from the rest of the animal kingdom is tenet of Judeo-Christianity. It was the belief that led (and still leads) white Europeans to oppress people of color by viewing them as "animals". There is absolutely no other way to dismantle white supremacy. As long as we try to affirm our "humanity" by trying to appeal the Colonial definition, we will always stay downtrodden.

Re/Considering Animals: A Black Woman's Journey

by Nekeisha A. Alexis

For the fate of humans and the fate of animals is the same; as one dies, so dies the other. They all have the same breath, and humans have no advantage over the animals; for all is vanity. All go to one place; all are from the dust, and all turn to dust again. Who knows whether the human spirit goes upward and the spirit of animals goes downward to the earth?

—Ecclesiastes 3:19–21 (New Revised Standard Version)

***

I am an animal liberationist.

Those are some of the words I use to express the view that other animals have beautiful and complex lives that are meaningful, good and worth preserving and respecting, regardless of their usefulness to humanity. It is my way of recognizing that other animals have their own intelligences, languages, skills, creativity, social landscapes, personalities, practices and spaces they call home; of declaring that each one is a unique, irreplaceable being whose dignity should be honored. The Christian tradition of which I am a part acknowledges that other animals are known individually and collectively by the Creator. As a result, I believe each of their lives should be valued — that their desires for joy, companionship, safety, wellness and freedom from unnecessary fear, suffering and trauma are legitimate. That our first posture toward them as neighbors should be generosity and grace: to do unto them what we would have done unto us. This perspective is fundamental to my adamant stance against subjecting other animals to exploitation, domination and wanton violence in all their industrial, technological, inter-personal, systemic and so-called humane forms. It is one of the reasons I reject using the overwhelming power we have accumulated as human animals to annihilate our most vulnerable kin.

At the core of this reorientation has been dismantling the faulty "human" vs. "animal" logic that underlies so much of our cruelty and disregard for other creatures. It has involved embracing the biological fact that we humans are a species of animal, not a group above or outside of that status, and discovering the biblical testimony that other animals are part of God's intention for right relationship, wholeness, justice and peace. Regardless of our shape or size or number of legs, we are all flesh carrying breath, tasked with fruitfulness in the broadest sense of the word.

Reconsidering animals from these vantage points as well as from my social location as a Black cisgender woman agitator living in the U.S. has led to a deeper and richer theology; a more empathetic living; a disruptive understanding of human being; and a revolutionary love for everybody. In this piece, I share some of the shifts I have made as I have gone from overlooking other animals as ethical and spiritual subjects to integrating them more fully into my consciousness. I offer these thoughts as an invitation, especially to other People of Color, to reconsider animals as well.

In the Beginning...

The movement toward this new outlook began in 2007, when I attended Wake Up Weekend at Calvin College in Grand Rapids, Michigan. The goal of this gathering was to raise awareness about the plight of nonhuman animals, especially those trapped in our industrial farming systems, and to promote veganism as a compassionate response to their conditions. At the time, the only vegans I remember coming across were two Jewish anarchists I met while living in New York City. Although my diet no longer included the carcasses of land animals and I called myself vegetarian, I was still eating fish and had no desire to abstain from all animal products. *If eating eggs and cheese didn't kill anybody, I* thought, *why be so extreme?*

At Wake-Up Weekend, I quickly discovered where the extremism really lies. Despite being in my mid-twenties, I still thought most animal-based products came from idyllic, "Old McDonald"-style farms with a cow, cow here and a chick, chick there. To be faced with the way 98% of flesh-foods arrived on U.S. tables— and, increasingly, on tables across the globe— undid me. The undercover footage of chickens with their necks wrapped around the bars of their unbearably-packed cages; workers slamming baby pigs head-first into concrete floors; sick and debilitated cows being dragged to the killing floor with tractors and chains; other animals being thrown around without care for injuries or broken limbs; and people taking great risks, enduring jail time and giving up their livelihoods to expose and stop this and other heinousness chilled and challenged the deepest parts of me.

One of the most powerful moments of the weekend for me occurred during a viewing of such footage. There was a scene in which cows who were no longer useful for milk production were being slaughtered. The video captured the complete anguish of the animals, and the scream-like bellows caused me to seize up in my chair and cover my eyes as I cried. Everything in me responded to their total despair and helplessness as people beat, kick, electric-shocked and forced these defenseless creatures toward a bloodbath. To see and hear such raw and senseless violence was bad enough; but to imagine myself as an animal victim whose entire life is pain, whose pain doesn't even count as legitimate, who is violated and abused without understanding why one is a target in the first place, added another layer of tragedy and sadism to the whole set up. My visceral response to this state of affairs affected me in a "Spirit groaning too deep for words" kind of way, and it's not an exaggeration to say I was compelled to become vegan by what I encountered. I knew that was the direction I had to move in, and steadily gave up my leftover habits in the following months.

Because of Wake-Up Weekend, I had several important realizations that helped me switch from animal-based foods and other products to plant-based living. The first was a simple admission: I had no idea this was happening. Billions of animals were undergoing this routine terror all over the planet, and I didn't have a clue. How was that possible? The second was a confession: My ignorance meant that I had been unwittingly complicit in a well-oiled machine of inconceivable violence. The cow who is forcibly impregnated, her milk stolen for human consumption, is the same cow who becomes hamburgers when she stops being "productive." The male calves who are born in order to produce milk in the first place are sold, chained and slaughtered for "veal." The eggs I was eating came from hatcheries where the male chicks are separated from the rest and then either ground-up alive or tossed into garbage bags and thrown into huge dumpsters, left to suffocate slowly. Vegans understood these cruelty connections across a variety of industries in a way my "eggs and milk don't kill" mentality had not, and they did their best to abstain as a matter of resistance.

My third response was incredulity at the widespread Christian silence on these issues. There I was: a proud pacifist, studying at a seminary with roots in a historic "peace church" tradition. Yet, up until that gathering, none of the faith communities I was part of— not even my fellow anti-war, nonviolence-advocating, social justice-oriented Mennonites— had lifted up this indiscriminate, unnecessary brutality as something we needed to confront as part of our witness. Our perspectives as Jesus-followers were so human-centered that the vast majority of us had disregarded one of the biggest death-machines of our day. Worse yet, when I began reasoning with other Christians about veganism, many of them justified subordinating other animals, readily admitted they didn't want to know or confessed that their love of a particular flesh-food was more important to them. I was so distraught by this disconnect that I used my studies to think theologically and ethically about other animals and the immoral situations in which we had placed them. That reflective work was essential for helping my veganism stick long after Wake Up Weekend was over.

Let There be Light

Just as my faith prompted me to become vegan, becoming vegan has also had profound and ongoing effects on my faith. One noteworthy change has been that I read the Bible differently. Indeed, the more I continued reading Scripture with sensitivity to other animals, the more I noticed how numerous the references are, and the surprising, sometimes contradictory, and unusual ways they appear. For example, the text describes other animals as moral agents (Jonah 3; Numbers 22:21-38), role models (Proverbs 6:6-11; Proverbs 30:24-28), and as having independent relationships with God (Psalm 104; Job 38-41). They are recipients of God's grace, provision and care (Psalm 104, 147; Job 38), and harmonious relationships with them are part of God's vision (Isaiah 11, 65).

This recognition is not unlike what happened when I began reading the Bible with feminist and womanist lenses and came to see a variety of portrayals. Just as the Bible has a mix of disturbing and affirming narratives about women, it also has disturbing and affirming narratives about other animals. Despite these diverse representations, many people— Christian and otherwise— act like the first and only word about other animals is "dominion," which has been devastatingly interpreted as license to indiscriminately use every nonhuman entity on Earth as we see fit. Yet very few people realize that, in the same creation narrative, dominion excludes eating other animals or that humans and other animals share the same substance and spirit. Similarly, many people are aware of texts that regulate animal sacrifice, but few know of those voices who spoke against the tradition— not on the grounds of contemporary animal rights discourse, of course, but because of God's ultimate desires for right worship, faithfulness, mercy and justice (Jeremiah 6, 7; Psalm 50; Amos 5; Micah 6; Matthew 12:1–9).

Another result of adopting veganism was seeing theological possibilities in places I previously had not. I'll offer two brief examples to illustrate this point. Christians often speak of salvation as an exclusively spiritual event for the benefit of some humans. However, Jesus's ending of all sacrifice means it is no longer necessary to kill other animals in order to commune and communicate with God; our worship need not be antagonistic toward or detrimental to other creatures (Hebrews 10:1–23). This is good news for other animals! What would it mean for Christians to take seriously this aspect of Jesus's saving work? Another example is the incarnation. A crucial part of Christian faith is the belief that God came as flesh and experienced flesh among us (John 1:1–14); but what does it mean that God's Spirit comes as a bird (Luke 3:2 – 22)? What might happen if Jesus-followers considered the implications of that visitation? Admittedly, neither of these examples on their own are enough to upend millennia of anthropocentric Christian theology; but I have found that there are more animal-friendly elements in Scripture than current one-dimensional interpretations allow, and those texts invite us into reformed relationships with them.

A third change has been that I value empathy and emotion as valid starting points for theology and ethics. In traditional Eurocentric/White-, male-dominated, classist academic spaces, these gifts are often met with suspicion or dismissed as unreliable sources for critical reflection. However, it was empathy that sparked my analysis and led me to adjust my behavior. I have also learned that, while empathy and emotion can expand our circles of care, that shift is not automatic. In fact, there are many instances when people who have been marginalized and oppressed do not recognize another community's marginalization and oppression, much less undertake the work to confront it. It takes a willingness to cross boundaries— an openness to look past predetermined, binary categories that separate us— to discover overlaps in our struggles and areas where mutual liberation is needed and possible.

And it Was So

In addition to my faith, my commitment to veganism was further sharpened and grounded by the work of theorists who recognized the connections between the normalized objectification and exploitation of other animals and the routine objectification and exploitation of dehumanized/animalized peoples. The first book that raised my awareness of these overlaps was Carol J. Adams's groundbreaking work, *The Sexual Politics of Meat: A Feminist Vegetarian Critique.*[1] Her book expanded my understanding of why who I consumed and how I thought about other animals mattered for me and other marginalized gendered (MaGe) persons in a patriarchal world. Her observation that flesh-food systems specifically target, control, and extract resources from bodies for their specific reproductive capabilities, is one I still find urgent. Adams's examination of common sexist images and language also showed the many ways European/Westernized cultures derogatorily animalize women and other MaGe. For example, think of the sexy womxn image, the purposeful innuendos in burger commercials, or even the use of terms like "bitch" or "pussy" as insults. In turn, we also find the sexualization of denigrated animals through the use of stereotypical "female" bodies (think of the sexy large breasted pig illustration on a barbecue menu and cases of workers actually sexually abusing hens). Unlike the majority of her peers, Adams identified how these cultural artifacts depended in part on the acceptance of literal violence through the non-male genderization of nonhuman animals to justify their exploitation and consumption in a patriarchal society, which follows male supremacy and depends on toxic masculinity to uphold it. The hen, sow, cow and MaGe are all abject in the dominant worldview, where all but cis men are ultimately disposable.

---

[1] I remain grateful to seminary colleague Brianne Donaldson for handing me Adam's book, ironically at an early morning Easter feast at a nearby Jesuit monastery.

However, most feminists do not pick up on this connection and end up supporting patriarchy and a culture of sexualized violence as a result.

In addition to Adams's work, Marjorie Spiegel's *The Dreaded Comparison: Human and Animal Slavery* was also instrumental for my early thinking on race and animals. One of her salient and lasting observations for me was that the tools and techniques plantation owners used against slaves, who were understood to be chattel, were also used in the process of domesticating laboring and farmed animals. Although I have since come to see flaws in Spiegel's approach in light of recent criticisms about making one-to-one comparisons between human and other animal suffering, the book did open me to consider the animal connections to European enslavement of African- and African-descended peoples in a way I previously had not. That openness helped me notice when theorists used their observations about other animals to build a case for biologically distinct races as I researched the development of race logic during the sixteenth to nineteenth centuries. It helped me see overlaps between nineteenth-century pro-slavery arguments and contemporary rationales for humane slaughter. It prompts me to think of what Delores S. Williams (1993) called the forced surrogacy of Black enslaved women —as wet nurses, as victims of rape, as denied mothers and their substitute mothering— and the status of lactating food animals. In these and other ways, integrating other animals into my analysis has transformed the way I think about race, and this has broadened my ideas on what undoing those constructs and dismantling their structures actually entails.

A third work that enhanced my explorations of gender, race and other animals is *Sistah Vegan: Black Female Vegans Speak on Food, Identity, Health and Society* by Dr. A. Breeze Harper. However, this anthology not only had an integrated approach to these topics; this approach was presented exclusively through the voices of other Black women. Here were personal stories told by people like me about adopting veganism for religious and spiritual reasons; for healing, self-determination and political empowerment; as an ecological imperative; for justice on behalf of other animals and Black, Brown and Indigenous peoples; from non-animal rights perspectives; and more. Some women reflected on living their ethics amidst skepticism and limited access to vegan resources. Others highlighted Black leaders that I had not previously heard of who had for decades advocated plant-based living as a means of Black survival and thriving. One of the lasting takeaways was editor A. Breeze Harper's point that, "Many people of color in African communities practiced plant-based holistic nutrition and herbalism" prior to colonization (2010, 37–38). This note, in addition to other historical and cultural information, challenged the idea of veganism as a White activity that opposes my identity and roots. Instead, *Sistah Vegan* placed veganism within older and current African-descended and Black traditions before me and helped me know I was not alone, despite being the only Black vegan of any gender in my immediate circles at the time.

Bring Forth Fruit

As is the case with many feminists, people of color and anti-racist activists often think about how White associations between us and other animals affects us. However, to conceive of Black people as deviant apes; or lazy "porch-monkeys;" or crows, jungle bunnies and bucks; and to maintain legal, social and political institutions based on our so-called less-than-humanness is not only a gross distortion of Black life and being. This conflation is also a gross distortion of primate persons and the other animal communities to whom we are compared. These mutually constituting and reinforcing lies all emerge from White supremacist, imperialist, colonialist approaches to non-European cultures and to the so-called natural world — and they create lethal consequences for all of us, across species. Although I understand why our struggle against antiblackness would be human-centered, I have come to see how we miss a significant piece of the framework that upholds our oppression in doing so. As Black Vegans Rock creator Aph Ko argues, we *can* consider other animals' liberation alongside ours: both their physical freedom *and* freedom from our conceptual constraints. To do otherwise is to fight only part of our battle.

Paying attention to the intersections between human oppression and the oppression of other animals has also enabled me to rethink prominent social justice issues. Slaughterhouses in the U.S. are an especially good example of this overlap. On one hand, these spaces are set up to destroy farmed individuals; but few people realize that, on the other hand, they are also racist, sexist, anti-worker and anti-immigrant. As the flesh-food industry has become bigger, faster and increasingly dangerous, its labor force has unsurprisingly shifted to more vulnerable populations and its working conditions have become more inhumane. Today, temporary and undocumented Latino/a/x immigrants make up a huge portion of slaughterhouse employees, in addition to refugees and underclass people of color and White people from the U.S. Industry giants actively recruit from Latin American countries and hire individuals without certainty about their citizenship status. This corporate strategy reduces the chance of worker organizing; suppresses complaints about abuses; keeps wages low; and allows employers to deny appropriate health care for the persistent injuries and disabilities that come with the job. Managers routinely engage in verbal and emotional abuse, humiliation, sexual harassment and bullying, and workers experience high rates of alcoholism, post-traumatic stress disorder and violence against their partners and in their households. It is no wonder that these workers do not speak up against cruelty when they see it or when they take out their frustrations on the farmed animals who are already marked as walking dead.

Factory farms are another example of these intersections. These sites of domination literally shit on economically-poor communities and communities of color at disproportionate rates compared to their White and affluent counterparts. North Carolina's Duplin and Sampson counties, "where 28 to 29 percent of residents live in poverty and a high proportion of residents are Black or Latino, host not only the largest numbers of

[Confined Animal Feeding Operations] in North Carolina, but in the entire country" (Cooke 2016). At the time of the report on this discrepancy, Duplin alone generated waste from 18.5 million farmed animals, and the state's operations were estimated to produce 10 billion gallons of wet fecal waste *every year* (Environmental Working Group 2016). A similar survey of Mississippi found that, of the 67 pig operations in the state, "the majority of the Mississippi's industrial hog operations are located in areas with high percentages of African Americans and persons in poverty" (Wilson 2002, 199). These agricultural nightmares produce lagoons of feces, spray waste onto neighboring properties, contaminate water sources and release toxic gases into the atmosphere, causing long-term health and ecological problems for residents.

Often, people of color are unaware that the baked goods we serve at our activist meetings or the chicken bodies we sell at our fundraisers or the charred pigs' flesh and cow's milk we have for breakfast are upholding some of the very same discriminations we contend with in other spheres. Funding these machines fuels the abuse of other animals *and* harms people like us the most.

And it Was Good

As a vegan and animal liberationist, I often run up against the belief that we can choose to help other animals or we can choose to help (our) people, but it's unreasonable or impossible to do both. We can fight for equal economic access and strive for prison abolition, or we can get distracted by dog rescues and conserving wildlife. What I have come to realize is that this is an artificial division; that many of the pressing issues we face are already interspecies concerns, even if we don't see them that way. The over-policing of Black communities is rooted in a centuries-old narrative of Black people as beasts— and of beasts as inconsequential. The U.S. military industrial complex that exerts power over other nations is also training dolphins, weaponizing dogs, using pigs for medical practice, and conducting experiments on hundreds of thousands of other animals ever year. The same struggle for indigenous rights in Brazilian rainforests is also a fight against industrial cattle ranching and meat exports to the U.S. When we become alert to the way oppressions affect all creatures, we can work more intentionally for the release of all involved.

Reconsidering other animals requires rethinking what it means to be human. This is a healthy challenge. As I accept that we are not as far from other animals, it forces me to reimagine what it is that makes me/us special and invites me to determine my/our worth in a way that is not oppositional and hierarchical. This invitation to be decentered— to recognize that the world as I know it is not the only world that matters— is a faith posture. However, it is also an important political position for me to take as I strive against dividing lines of hostility and work toward a life more abundantly for all.

Ultimately, my practice of veganism and identity as animal liberationist grows out of radical, generous love. I hope you will consider this path for your life, for our lives and for everyone's futures.

Cited Works

Adams, C. J. (2002). *The Sexual Politics of Meat: A Feminist Vegetarian Critique. Tenth Anniversary Edition*. Continuum, New York.

Cattle Ranching in the Amazon Region. *Global Forest Atlas*. Yale University. Accessed December 31, 2018: https://globalforestatlas.yale.edu/amazon/land-use/cattle-ranching

Cooke, C. (2016). North Carolina's Factory Farms Produce 15,000 Olympic Pools Worth of Waste Each Year. *Civil Eats*. Accessed December 31, 2018: http://civileats.com/2016/06/28/north-carolinas-cafos-produce-15000-olympic-size-pools-worth-of-waste/

Compa, L. (2004). *Blood, sweat, and fear: Workers' rights in U.S. meat and poultry plants*. New York, NY: Human Rights Watch. Accessed December 31, 2018: http://digitalcommons.ilr.cornell.edu/reports/331/

Conover, T. (2013). The way of all flesh: Undercover in an industrial slaughterhouse. *Harper's Magazine*, 31–49.

Durand, A. (2004). *Wegman's Cruelty*. [Motion picture]. United States: Compassionate Consumers.

Environmental Working Group. (2016). Exposing Fields of Filth: Landmark Report Maps Feces-Laden Hog and

Chicken Operations in North Carolina. Accessed December 31, 2018: https://www.ewg.org/research/exposing-fields-filth

Genoways, T. (February 2013). This land is not your land: Deciding who belongs in America. *Harper's Magazine*, 33–41.

Harper, A. B. (2010). Social Justice Beliefs and Addiction to Uncompassionate Consumption. In A. B. Harper (Ed.) *Sistah Vegan: Black Female Vegans Speak on Food, Identity, Health and Society* (20–41). Lantern Books, Brooklyn.

Hediger, R. (2013) Animals and War: Introduction. In R. Hediger (Ed.) *Animals and War: Studies of Europe and North America* (1–25). Brill, Lieden.

Ko, A. (2017). #ALLVEGANSROCK: The All Lives Matter Hashtag of Veganism. *Aphro-ism: Essays on Pop Culture, Feminism, and Black Veganism from Two Sisters* (13–19). Lantern Books, Brooklyn.

Laveck, J. and Stein. J. (2012). *Peaceable Kingdom: The Journey Home* [Motion picture]. United States: A Tribe of Heart Documentary.

Moritz. J. M. (2009). Animals and the Image of God in the Bible and Beyond. *Dialog: A Journal of Theology*, 48(2), 134–146.

Nebraska Appleseed (2009). *The Speed Kills You: The Voice of Nebraska's Meatpacking Workers*. Lincoln.

Accessed December 31, 2018:
https://neappleseed.org/wp-content/uploads/downloads/2013/01/the_speed_kills_y ou_100410.pdf

Spiegel, M. (1996). *The Dreaded Comparison: Human and Animal Slavery. Revised and Expanded Edition.* Mirror Books, New York.

Williams, Delores S. (1993). *Sisters in the Wilderness: The Challenge of Womanist God-Talk*, Orbis Books, New York.

Wilson, S. M., Howell, F., Wing, S. & Sobsey, M. (2002). Environmental Injustice and the Mississippi Hog Industry. *Environmental Health Perspectives, 100*(Suppl 2), 195–201. Accessed December 31, 2018: https://www.ncbi.nlm.nih.gov/pmc/articles/PMC1241116 3/pdf/ehp110s-000195.pdf

Veganism as a Liberating, Anti-Oppressive Practice

By Jocelyn Ramirez

I remember crying in a corner at the age of four at the thought of death. How could it be that everyone and every living being would eventually die? I remember thinking about my parents, my sisters, and nonhuman animals dying. My love for horses and pandas is what I remember most from my childhood innocence.

People often say children are innocent and have yet to learn the harsh realities of life, but I knew then what it felt like to hear how nonhuman animals and the Earth are exploited for no reason. Most importantly, I thought that "bad people" – people separate from my world and I – were the ones who were carrying out this violence in the world. I did not think of myself or my loved ones as exploiters of other peoples, communities, and nonhuman animals; it was up to us "good people" to stop this exploitation. I felt that people did not care about this exploitation of the Earth and her animals, because if people did care, then why was this pain and suffering allowed to continue? Why did people not feel the same urgency to do *anything* that I felt?

I did not make the connection of this exploitation to diet until I was almost twenty years old. I always tell people that I did not intentionally become vegan. I would keep the booklets that vegans and vegetarians would hand out outside of my high school, with the hope that one day I could become a vegetarian. In part, what held me back was that it was hard for me to imagine what that would look like, as I was raised in a Mexican-American household. My family's diet consisted of *arrachera, barbacoa, carnitas, pollo, chorizo, chuletas,* and *carne molida.* In other words, a lot of fucking dead animals.

After a period of depression and anxiety, there was a lot of food that I stopped enjoying. During this same time, I began cultivating my foundation for social justice, rooted in the Black Lives Matter movement and the reproductive justice movement. I grew exasperated and enraged at the violence, displacement, and marginalization from not just the criminal (in)justice system, but the local and national government as well, wondering: Why are they not protecting us young, poor, queer, or disabled People of Color? I soon came to realize that the very institutions I was hoping could help us were born out of the same violence that I was hoping they would stop. For many activists, confronting oppression can feel hopeless most of the time. I was left exhausted and frustrated. One day, I opened the fridge and realized that I had not eaten meat in two days, so I challenged myself to see how long I could last. After two weeks, I decided that vegetarianism was not enough and decided to go vegan.

While I intended to challenge myself and eat for my health, a part of me was striving to live according to the social justice values I was cultivating– and am still cultivating. My diet and other consumption choices thus became very *intentional*. I didn't see myself as a "good" or "bad" person but as someone who both struggles against and benefits from the systems of oppression. From the ages of 20-23, I consistently grew in my analyses and consciousness. At age four, my analysis of animal exploitation was, "I don't want animals to die." Although my first step towards veganism was related to diet, it has since extended beyond plant-based eating. Now I can say that animal exploitation– animal oppression– is perpetuated by white supremacy, ableism, capitalism, colonization, and cisheteropatriachy. Try saying that in one second– a mouthful, for sure. I also now understand how the relationships between People of Color and nonhuman animals have changed due to these systems of oppression, and I am thankful for Black feminists and scholars like siblings Aph and Syl Ko, Christopher Sebastian, and Dr. A. Breeze Harper in furthering my anti-racist and anti-oppressive analysis for nonhuman animals.

If we look deeper, it becomes clear that nonhuman animals are oppressed through the same systems that People of Color are oppressed. I see this in the ways that nonhuman animals are used to serve white supremacy and imperialism through the police and military (Salter et al. 2015), in the same ways that People of Color are conditioned to help these institutions (Christensen 2016). I see this in the ways that nonhuman animals are used in medicinal experiments, in the same vein that People of Color, people with disabilities, women, and poor people and their bodies were – are – used to serve the medical-industrial complex (Roberts 2012). I see this in the way that nonhuman animals are forced to migrate because, just like People of Color, they have been colonized and displaced (Brownlow 2000).

If nonhuman animals and their bodies are exploited, used, and displaced, how is it that they are not an oppressed community in the same vein that queer/LGBTQ+ communities, disabled communities, Communities of Color and women are oppressed? Nonhuman animals are also sentient and have families, language, and culture. Oppressed people do not have their humanity recognized. We, People of Color, routinely experience this. We, as oppressed beings ourselves, have also failed to extend personhood to nonhuman animals.

Thus, I ask my fellow communities to hold ourselves accountable to nonhuman animals and the Earth. Every day, we, People of Color, are denied our humanity; but, as we fight for the liberation of all oppressed people, we must not fall victim to a type of liberation that is rooted in the humanization of wealthy, white, non-disabled, heterosexual men. Fighting for freedom requires finding solidarity with all who are oppressed under the same system, including nonhuman animals. We cannot defeat oppressive systems without addressing justice for nonhuman animals because their oppression is deeply entrenched in the systems that directly oppress human animals. Intersectionality, the theory coined by Kimberlé Crenshaw, provides us with a framework in understanding oppression: racism, heterosexism, ableism, speciesism, and all other systems of marginalization are interconnected and work to reinforce one another mutually. In the words of Audre Lorde, "There is no such thing as single-issue struggles because we do not live single-issue lives." Nonhuman animal exploitation is interconnected with the oppression of human animals.

Veganism for me is not about diet. It is about living and striving for social justice for all communities. Social justice inherently includes identifying and admitting that nonhuman animals are beings also living in colonized, oppressed bodies. I have no intention of going back to a non-vegan lifestyle. Liberation for us all is not about guilt or competition with other forms of liberation. It is about recognizing that if we want to achieve social justice – liberation - we must fight – love - for everyone, or we will never find true justice.

I hope that my four-year-old self would be proud of the person that I am today. I am critical of the ways that children's thoughts and emotions are ignored just because of their status as children. What would it have meant for my four-year-old self to have my concerns about violence towards animals acknowledged and validated by adults? To have had my worries met with respect and dignity? I think she would be happy to know that living free from nonhuman animal exploitation, even in a Mexican household, is quite easy.

Cited Works

Brownlow, A. (2000). A Wolf in the Garden Ideology and Change in the Adirondack Landscape. *In* Philo, C. and Wilbert, C. (Eds.), *Animal Spaces, Beastly Places*. Routledge, London.

Christensen, W. M. (2016). The Black Citizen-Subject: Black Single Mothers in US Military Recruitment Material. *Ethnic and Racial Studies*, 39(14), 2508-2526. doi:10.1080/01419870.2016.1160139

Roberts, D. (2012). *Fatal Invention: How Science, Politics, and Big Business Re-create Race in the Twenty-First Century*. New Press, New York.

Salter, C., Nocella, A. J., Bentley, J. K., & McCarthy, C. (2015). *Animals and war: Confronting the military-animal industrial complex*. Lexington Books, Lanham.

Outsiders: Finding Community through Connected Experiences

By Namita Money

I went vegan after learning about the objectification and commodification that is inherent in the farming of nonhuman animals. It was a step for me to more closely align my actions with my morals. For as long as I can remember, I have always had better relationships with, and felt more connected to, nonhuman animals than humans. I just feel the most comfortable around those who have fur, scales, or feathers.

Growing up as a second-generation Indian in the predominantly-white suburb of Rochester Hills, Michigan, I was accustomed to feeling like an outsider. Quite frankly, I was embarrassed by my culture, and I strove to assimilate to whiteness. I felt great shame that my food never looked or smelled like the perfectly-cut white-bread sandwiches that my peers would bring in their lunchboxes. I refused to wear a *pottu* to school, for fear of standing out even more than I already did. I was very observant of my parents turning on a "US American accent" when around white people. I learned to revile Indian accents and what they stood for, and, although I adored the Indian clothes my grandmother and mother bought for me, we made sure to reserve these for Indian occasions only. I strongly believe that these experiences of not fitting in shaped my love of and connection to nonhuman animals. Both of us were misunderstood, our diversity ignored by mainstream culture. There didn't seem to be a space carved out for us. I felt solidarity with these beings, whose beauty, resilience, and passion for life truly inspire me. Despite their conditions, they have endless love and happiness to offer to the world.

After learning about the horrific and cruel practices of the dairy and egg industries in high school, my sister and I decided to go vegan together. Having been raised as a vegetarian with the ideal that all animals deserve respect and compassion, it was unfathomable to me how carelessly humans treated factory farmed animals. I was utterly confused by how we could act so ruthlessly towards these beings, who are very clearly sentient and capable of feeling emotions. Above all, I was shocked by how humans claim to understand the intelligence of other species, yet continuously come back to the same conclusion that we are the most superior species just so that we can justify our continual exploitation of them.

In college, I wanted to do more, so I turned to nonhuman animal rights activism and volunteering to help animals in my community at local animal sanctuaries. I had the amazing opportunity to build relationships with farmed animals and rescued "exotic" pets who had been abandoned when their guardians realized that they were, in fact, neither dogs nor cats.

The bonds that I formed with these beloved beings were a constant reminder of why being vegan mattered to me as an ethical stance. These animals had dealt with so much adversity in their lives as a result of humans.

During my activism in college, I learned a great deal about the animal advocacy movement, and because of our long-standing animal rights club, I had the opportunity to meet many leaders in the activism movement. For these experiences, I am truly grateful. However, towards the end of my time in college, I began to feel disillusioned by the activism I was doing. It felt strange to me that most of the activists I encountered were white, when I knew from my own culture that the ideas behind veganism were certainly not invented by white folks. Now I know more about the erasure of vegans of color by the mainstream vegan movement and about the way in which adopting a vegan lifestyle is an act of decolonization, as well as a move towards going back to the roots of our ancestors. It has also become clear to me that the methods used by the mainstream animal rights movement are not effective in communities of color, where lack of access of fresh fruits and vegetables is the norm, overlapping systems of oppression have ruined our health and our relationships with nonhuman animal communities, and where there is a general mistrust of white people. It felt to me like I was participating in methods of advocacy that perpetuated the oppression of humans, rather than exposing the connections between injustices inflicted upon humans and nonhuman animals.

I have now chosen to leave many mainstream activism spheres because of the damage I see them inflicting on marginalized people, which I do not find effective in growing a larger compassion-based movement for nonhuman animals. To me, it has become incredibly clear that the way our colonized society treats our fellow humans and the way we treat other species is connected.

My veganism is rooted in the astounding interspecies friendships that I have had the privilege of forming with so many victims of industrial farming. It is my love and respect for nonhuman animals that drives my passion for helping them and fighting for their rights. However, I do not believe that one must particularly love nonhuman animals in order to wish them a life free from suffering, harm, and objectification. People of color in the United States, a colonized land, have less privilege than white folks. We know what it is like to not be taken seriously because of our background, ethnicity, or the color of our skin. In the same system that calls us outsiders and points fingers at us, nonhuman animals, too, are seen as lesser beings. They struggle to exist in a world dominated by humans, in which it is humans who decide their fates—where they can and cannot exist, the size of their communities, etc.— and humans who are rapidly destroying their environment and uprooting their homes. In the same *cis-tem* that has oppressed us into thinking that our cultures and identities are unwelcome and are just not "right," nonhuman animals are refused the right to their bodily autonomy because of the mere fact that they are of a different species. Being anything other than food, fur, skin, entertainment, or an object on which to be tested is simply unacceptable.

Veganism comes from the realization that nonhuman animals have the right to exist on Earth just as much as we humans do. Although the vegan movement is unique in that it is a social justice movement that is not led by its victims, it is a movement founded on the ideals of anti-oppression. As members of marginalized and minoritized groups, we people of color are uniquely able to widen our circles of compassion to include nonhuman animals, who are also marginalized. We know what it is to fight against the system every day, by our mere existence. If we dig just a little bit deeper within ourselves, we will find that the depersonification that we experience and the depersonification of nonhuman animals are actually connected under the cis imperialist white supremacist capitalist patriarchy in which we live.

Of course, I would be remiss if I did not address the elephant in the room— the main reason for which people of color are turned off by the mainstream vegan movement. The movement, like many justice move-ments, has unfortunately been wrought by ableism, sexism, racism, classism, homophobia, and transphobia.

Yet, the root of veganism itself is centered on compassion and kindness. How can the mainstream movement stray so far from this baseline?

I can't answer for the mainstream movement, but my veganism is one led by vegans of color. It involves acknowledging and standing in solidarity with other social justice movements, resisting the oppression of both humans and nonhumans, and working to create veganism that is accessible to all. My veganism includes human animals just as much as it does nonhuman animals. In the veganism I aspire for our world, no group of people is oppressed, regardless of their species, race, gender, sex, size, abilities, culture, or class.

The Hope and Promise of Sanctuary

by Kamekə Brown

I recently attended an event at East Bay Meditation Center (EBMC)—a community meditation center in Oakland, California created to be a welcoming space for underrepresented communities and to foster "liberation, personal and interpersonal healing, social action, and inclusive community building."[1] The event, called "#MuditaRevolution: Cultivating the Heart of Joy to Counteract Capitalism," focused on exploring alternatives to capitalism through heart-based practices such as *mudita*, which is often described as finding joy in appreciating the well-being and good fortune of others– empathetic joy. It centered on how shifting from a focus on accumulation of material to celebrating the joy of connection and community can be a revolutionary act, propelling us in the direction of resilience and liberation. Through discussion, guided meditation, and various activities, we reflected on our experiences of capitalism and how we can engage in practices to envision and embody counter-capitalist alternatives.

During the event, attendees were read a section from *Octavia's Brood: Science Fiction Stories from Social Justice Movements* (Walidah and Brown 2015), an anthology of fictional tales from activists and organizers that bring to life visions of a future beyond the oppressive systems of our current world through the use of radical imagination. The section we were read was titled "Letter from Alexis after Capitalism to Alexis during

Capitalism." It detailed the contents of a letter of encouragement that a character in the text, Alexis, writes to their past self from the future, describing the joy and wellness of the post-capitalist world for which past-Alexis was fighting. The letter offered hope and reassurance based not on unfounded or empty promises, but on a vision that had become a true reality and was presently being experienced by future-Alexis.

After we were read the letter, we were given a few minutes to write a version of the letter for ourselves.

I chose to write about sanctuary:

> Dear Kamekə,
>
> Hey you. There was a poem you started once and never quite finished. It's possible that you don't remember it, but I do. In it, you said, "I need to know that I survive this" for the child that you once were and everything she deserves—all of the hopes you have for her. I remember the time you were in when you wrote it. I remember Dawn. I remember Linus, Gus, Petunia, Joan, and all of the lives and loves of that time and place. Sanctuary. You wanted to believe in a future where these relationships are as beautiful, real, and _priceless_ as the moments you all shared with one another. You wanted to believe in a future that fulfilled and outshone the promise and potential of this place. It exists. You'll survive this. Sanctuary is real. You'll see.

I chose to write about sanctuary because "sanctuary" is where I work and where I have lived for the past several years. The sanctuary that I am referring to is a farmed animal sanctuary. Farmed animal sanctuaries are intended to be spaces where individuals of farmed animal species– who come from situations of abuse, neglect, and where they would be used solely for human purposes – can live their lives free from further abuse, neglect, use, and exploitation. Within sanctuary spaces, I have witnessed the transformative power of relationships, the beauty and potential of a commitment to the practice of mudita, and the alternative worlds we can create when we prioritize community and connection over profit and material.

In the United States, it is commonplace that farmed animals are bred and raised to be used solely for human purposes. Their lives are considered to be inferior and their interest in living is believed to be unimportant. It is the norm in the United States that humans exert full control over farmed animals' lives: breeding them to have certain qualities for human benefit, structuring their lives and disrupting their relationships to satisfy human wants, and, ultimately, exercising power to end their lives as we see fit so that we can consume and use their bodies.

It is the norm in our society to walk into a grocery store and to see and be able to buy the bodies of farmed animals. It is the norm in our society to use products made from animal flesh and animal secretions.

Farmed animal sanctuaries are powerful counter-capitalist spaces in the ways that they seek to transform the relationships of commodification and exploitation that we have with farmed animals under capitalism in the United States to relationships of care— relationships that respect and affirm an individual's right to their body and life, regardless of that individual's species. Under capitalism, an individual matters only insofar as they are able to contribute to profitable outcomes. The primary consideration individuals, human and nonhuman, are given within capitalist systems is in regard to how they can be used and exploited to benefit the system (and those at the top of it). Care, community, connection, and empathy are viewed as hindrances in a profit-driven world that calls for the privileging of efficiency and mass production at lowest possible cost, with greatest possible financial outcome.

Sanctuaries counter that notion by shifting the focus from how farmed animals' bodies and lives can be financially profitable to any human to how humans can best contribute to farmed animals' wellbeing. Sanctuaries provide a space for farmed animals to live their lives for no purpose other than their own, and sanctuary volunteers and employees rejoice in seeing those individuals living with as much freedom, wellness, and agency as possible—the embodiment of empathetic joy.

It is because of Sanctuary that I first got to know and build relationships with farmed animals –individuals who I had only really previously encountered as bodies made available for me to use and consume on a dinner plate. Through Sanctuary, I built relationships with individuals like a pig we call Lola, who is always eager for belly rubs and content to be snuggled up with the rest of the sounder.

I got to know a cow named Betsy, who is fiercely protective of her family and always loving and patient with the antics of the younger members of her herd. She is the mother I aspire to be.

I got to know a pig named Maya: a trauma survivor, resilient and full of life, even as she forever carried the scars and neurotic habits that alluded to her difficult past.

In Sanctuary, these are individual recipients and givers of care— not tools or products. Sanctuary is a space where I learned the transformative power of priceless relationships of care, love, and respect, and how such power can be wielded as a radical form of anti-capitalist resistance.

In a world in which those who are oppressed and disenfranchised are not only not expected to survive but also actively *prevented* from surviving, a space that asserts their right to exist, thrive, and have agency and sovereignty over their own bodies is a profoundly liberating one. When I first experienced Sanctuary, I knew there was something powerful about a space that gives beings a place to live and be cared for and respected when the world beyond that space is intent upon their demise. In ways that I did not expect and am learning more about every day, Sanctuary is a space in which I have found solidarity and healing.

As a queer Black woman, I know something about the struggles of navigating a world characterized by a set of assumptions about my worth, my value, and the entitlement of others to my labor and my body. To exist in a space that seeks to reject the notion that the lives and bodies of others are ours to use as we wish was the actualization of a hope that I had yet to encounter elsewhere to the same degree. I have met and loved many others who I know have found a similar hope, peace, and healing in this place. My commitment to sanctuary is an act of solidarity– a commitment to co-liberation. It is often said that "existence is resistance;" I've learned sanctuary to be the manifestation of that.

Within sanctuary, I learned what it means to grieve the loss of those whose lives are not considered to be of value and whose deaths aren't considered grievable. Dawn (a cow), Linus (a cow), Gus (a goat), Petunia (a sheep), Joan (a pig), and my dear human friend, Nic– in Sanctuary, their lives mattered, and so did their deaths. We grieved them and are still grieving them every day.

Billions of farmed animals are slaughtered for food annually in the United States, and their deaths are celebrated for how their bodies will be used rather than grieved for the individuals they were. In sanctuary, I began to fully reject that erasure and allow myself to grieve the loss of Black and Brown bodies, queer bodies, and the bodies of marginalized folx whose lives and deaths are overlooked. I learned to allow myself to feel the true magnitude of that loss, and to understand that depth of feeling as an act of solidarity, love, and resistance.

That grief has felt heavy, I'll admit– a weight I haven't always been sure I could carry or survive; but the promise and potential of Sanctuary offers hope that a different world is possible, and that creating it is within reach.

Sanctuary helped me realize just how much power we have to embrace a counter-oppressive future *now*, rather than in some distant future. When I envisioned who and where I would be post-capitalism– in a more counter-oppressive future– I envisioned a world of Sanctuary, fulfilled. When I reflected on mudita and embodying empathetic joy, I contemplated the moments of love, care, relationship, and healing I have shared with my sanctuary community. My experiences of Sanctuary have highlighted the potential of what we can create and cultivate, even in an oppressive world; and that those spaces of hope and potential are where we plant and witness the seeds of our future. I have witnessed that that future is most beautiful, most healing, most transformative when it reflects a commitment to co-liberation and rejects any notion that suggests that "Your body is mine to use as I please" or "Your life matters less, or not at all."

Sanctuary is real. It exists. Trust me. You'll see.

Cited Works

Walidah, I. and Brown, A. (2015). *Octavias Brood: Science Fiction Stories from Social Justice Movements*. AK Press, Oakland, CA.

Unlearning Life-Long Lessons

By Kez St. Louis

My method of understanding is usually through mentally putting myself in others' situation, especially since marginalized people have a common experience of being disadvantaged by systems of oppression, and I, myself, am in a marginalized position. I am a queer and Black trans vegan.

I don't want to force someone else who is not ready for my specific kind of thought process to engage in it, as I don't want to cause feelings of hurt by opening wounds, if that makes sense. However, I'm in the part of my journey as someone committed to speaking up against all forms of oppression and their interconnections that, if you are open to it, I do want to share my thoughts, because these conversations are important.

Simply stated, speciesism is an often-ignored form of bigotry against nonhuman animals that upholds the idea that humans are superior to all other animals. This is something we, marginalized People of Color, must unlearn.

On my way to work, I've encountered a specific advertisement many times. Each time I see it, it makes me think that it is so blatantly bigoted that it's almost incredible that it is even in use. The advert says, "Stand up straight. Your humanity is at stake." It then shows an image of a hunched-over gorilla.

This message exemplifies how speciesism and capitalism, a system that prioritizes profit and commodifies living beings (humans and nonhumans alike), are often employed simultaneously to influence our choices. Capitalism typically has a heavy hand in perpetuating bigotry– particularly bigotry against all marginalized persons, which includes nonhuman animals– in order to sell to those who have the most worth and capital in society. This why veganism is much more than what you have in your pot, on your plate, or in your fridge. It is, first and foremost, what you consume in the mind.

Veganism is, among other things, the adoption of the mentality that living beings are not objects. Mainstream capitalist society feeds your mind messages that nonhuman animals are lesser than humans, and, because they are lesser than, they are "things" to be exploited and abused and tortured and overlooked and discarded and used for the entertainment of humans. This while simultaneously elevating and idealizing humanness, even though human workers in a capitalist system are similarly othered to objectify them as production units and nothing more. Society tells us that we are better than and stronger than; and that if we *can* dominate them, we should. Humans created this divide: the notion that we, humans, are disconnected from our animality and nature, and that we are above those things. We uphold this false dichotomy/false binary of human and animal. However, plainly stated, this is simply a system of oppression meant to control other a-nimals and justify the atrocities we commit against them.

This same system promotes a conception of "humanness" that implies whiteness, able-bodiedness and neurotypicalness, as well as straightness, cisness, and even wealth (especially generational wealth). It's a system that exploits all of us who are not deemed worthy of this type of humanness. It's important to note that there is a difference between paralleling experiences and direct comparisons of experiences. There is a formula of oppression used in the oppression of both nonhuman animals and marginalized humans, one that includes otherization and the creation of imaginary hierarchies, and so, the further we look between interconnections, we find that oppression is not exclusive to the human experience.

Going back to the advertisement, the image primarily puts down gorillas, as they are a species that is genetically close to humans but are seen as primitive to humans. They are seen as an example of where humans came from and how we evolved and are now; however, this ideology robs gorillas of their own personhood, unrelated to ours, as different beings with their own community, language, survival skills, customs, needs, etc. The way in which society deems that they do not have worth when held up to the standard of humanness means that it is easy to justify their oppression and accept it.

Once you begin to see what is wrong with the advertisement featuring the gorilla being compared to the human (apart from the obvious ableism, which is another system of oppression; the ad implies that humans who cannot stand up straight are somehow inferior to those who can), those thoughts are vegan thoughts.

If you ever were upset or angry after watching *Blackfish* because of the horrible conditions killer whales endure, those thoughts are vegan thoughts. If you have ever thought to yourself, nonhuman animals should not be in cages, those thoughts are vegan thoughts. If you've ever thought we should not hit animals, starve animals, or displace animals— *** all of those thoughts are vegan thoughts***.

These thoughts are not white-only thoughts or thoughts reserved only for dominant, privileged groups. If you consistently apply these beliefs to the rest of your life and let them guide you, you already understand how to add veganism to your fight for justice.

Although it is a life-long journey of unlearning, as with any form of oppression we have been indoctrinated into, I promise you, we are all in this, as even vegans who go vegan overnight constantly work against their own speciesism in a world that normalizes it— just as it normalizes our own oppression. In truth, **veganism isn't a destination; it's a direction.** You keep going as far *as is practicable and possible* for you in order to be in solidarity with other beings on this planet every time you get the chance. This is why people who eat plant-based aren't always vegans. It's an ideology, first. It's how you see the world. Even what you eat is a much larger issue than what you eat. Why? Think about it: When someone says someone is a pig, ask yourself why you would equate pigs with something negative. When someone says, it's just a chicken, ask yourself why that chicken is an "it" to them, and what about being a chicken makes them someone who doesn't deserve to live. When someone says that someone "lost their humanity," really analyze what that person lost and why you equate those traits to being inherently and exclusively human traits. These thoughts will feed you well, as they will help you make the connections needed to take a hard stance against systemic oppression in order to truly nourish all the beings around you.

We Can Do It All

By Jael A'sa Israel

Asking for emotional labor to oppose the oppression of other animals whilst we, ourselves, are oppressed is a hard ask, but it is not beyond the realms of possibility. Poverty, racism, xenophobia, ableism, classism, misogyny, capitalism, food insecurity, and all other forms of oppression are interlinked. They have a common driving force, our common enemy: white, patriarchal supremacy.

Dismantling this oppressive system that is holding us all back is beneficial for humans and non-human animals alike. No one for one second is comparing our suffering to the suffering of other animals; but we are all suffering together, at the same time, under the same system. If the system falls, marginalized peoples will gain their freedom, and other species will also gain theirs. Call me an idealist, but surely that outcome is one for which we should all strive?

I am acutely aware of all of the hurdles that lie in our wake. Food insecurity, food deserts, struggling households, poverty, poor housing, underfunded education systems, under and unemployment, a criminal justice system that preys on and terrorizes Black and Brown bodies, lack of access, lack of voice and poor infrastructure plague our communities, all of which are not of our doing and in many cases, beyond our control. As we work to break down these barriers, we enter a world in which all oppression, wherever it is found, is challenged and dismantled simultaneously. Even if non-human animal freedom is not at the forefront of your thoughts and actions, minimizing your part in another species's suffering whilst reducing the money spent propping up animal agriculture and financing our oppressors can be done alongside the fight for our own liberation.

In developed nations, up to two-thirds of total cereal production is used as animal feed (Erb et al. 2012), whilst the vast majority of our brothers and sisters in developing countries starve from a lack of food. The oppression of nonhuman animals (rearing them for meat, milk, eggs, wool, honey, silk) is tied closely to PoC (People of Color) suffering and experiencing poverty. It is mainly our people who work in abattoirs and on farms, whilst not being paid fairly for their labor. The West consumes large quantities of luxury food items (sugar, spices, coffee, chocolate, quinoa, avocados) which People of Color are not adequately compensated for producing. We have cheaply-manufactured products because People of Color are in a field or a factory, slaving away for tuppence. Who is responsible for this? The white supremacist patriarchy. How will this system end? By us working together to dismantle it, brick by brick, system by system oppression by oppression.

"Veganism" is a concept that is barely 74 years old and was born out of a colonial language and theory to which many of us feel alien; but People of Color (for centuries, millennia, or however you see time) have lived a non-oppressive, non-violent existence before the systems of white supremacy uprooted us from or enslaved us within our native and indigenous lands. Some of us may have lost our native tongues, in which we could accurately describe this existence; but I long for us to rediscover our former history and return to living in a cohesive, empathic, harmonious society, in which we are at one with nature and each other and in which no species is abused, maltreated or utilized as a commodity.

The modern, rabid consumption of meat is a post-colonial legacy and one which we (melanated beings) have not profited from as a people. The vast majority of our traditional, indigenous foods are plant-based, and animals were a sign of our great wealth and compassion. Even when meat was eaten historically, it most certainly did not make up a large portion of every meal, and animals were not systemically violated to the same degree as they are now. "Vegan" food (in the European 70-something-year-old sense of the term) has been co-opted and gentrified and has become very expensive and thus, not widely accessible. However, many of our traditional foods are predominantly plant-based and, to many of us, they are still affordable.

I am hyper-sensitive of my privilege of living in the U.K., where I am not located in or near a food desert; where I have access to supermarkets that sell fruits, vegetables, grains, and seeds; where I have access to and the financial freedom to purchase items that do not contain animal by-products; and, having choice and agency, where I also have the luxury of time and the emotional and intellectual space required to live a plant-based existence. If you, like me, are part of the privileged poor, you, too can utilize some of that privilege to make a change to your way of life. We can also work hard to eliminate the barriers which prevent our brothers and sisters from making the same change.

"Veganism" is not our movement, nor is it the end goal; it is merely a starting point to incorporate the liberation of non-human animals into our collective fight for freedom. I, personally, will never center white people or their theories in any movement or activism in which I participate. We know they are problematic, we know that they can never truly be allies, we know they will spend their emotional energy on everybody and everything but us; but WE, as oppressed groups, can clearly see and identify other forms of oppression when we see it. We can see the nuances and the interrelation of oppression, and as we are bringing down the system that has us in a bind, the animals will be liberated too. If you have the emotional capacity and ability to do so, please consider an anti-oppression, multifaceted, inter-sectional approach to your fight for freedom.

Cited Works

Erb, K.H., Mayer, A., Kastner, T., Sallet, K.E., and Haberl, H. (2012). *The Impact of Industrial Grain Fed Livestock Production on Food Security: an extended literature review.* Compassion in World Farming, The Tubney Charitable Trust, and World Society for the Protection of Animals, UK. Vienna, Austria.

Rejecting the Master's Playbook
Ensuring Our Own Liberation FROM White Supremacy

By Danielle Moore

As a black person, I am at the point in my journey where I can freely admit that other animals are not "other" to us. We are them, and they are us. As black people, we won't liberate ourselves by putting ourselves at the top and others at the bottom. In order to achieve black liberation, we need different tools from the "master's." We need not **become** master.

I have spent my life as a black woman being animalized by white people from the time I started interacting with them. My father was called a monkey by my mom's family, even before my birth. I know what it means to be *otherized* and *animalized* by white supremacist ideology. From the agricultural revolution and U.S. slavery, the root of oppression befalling upon me, my ancestors, and nonhuman farmed animals can be traced back to white supremacist and capitalist values— the use of others' bodies for personal (rich, white) gain. Along my journey, I came to the realization that the comparison of black people to nonhuman animals was and is still used as a tool to divide us from them and make us into a "lesser" being. When we accept that our oppressors, white people, use this othering as a tool to keep us oppressed, it becomes clear that we must reject this tool for ourselves. To me, it has become vital that we embrace our shared struggles with nonhumans and rise up together against these tools upholding the ideals that have forced us into this oppressive relationship in the first place.

As black humans, we do face incomparable oppression to other human communities, but we do not face the particular system of oppression that falls on nonhuman animals. No matter how hard we are fighting for our lives as black people, other animals are *still* routinely held against their will, stolen from their families, eaten alive, having their body fluids stolen in painful and permanently-damaging ways, and being murdered for their bodies. The choice of being complicit or not in nonhuman animal oppression is a human privilege. We, even black people, have this privilege. We all have the energy to, at the very least, recognize that we, ourselves, are complicit in oppression, and we can choose not to be complicit through our everyday choices.

"If I am going to be oppressed, then I don't have to care about others who I oppress" is not how compassion and justice work. If we look at examples of black capitalists, we can see that, while many of them have climbed to "the top," they act in oppressive ways towards folks (including other black folks) they see as "other." This shows that when mindsets and systems work in oppressive and exploitative ways, we will never be free from the chance of becoming otherized ourselves. We would maximize our own freedoms by fighting for all creatures – human and nonhuman. As black humans, liberating everyone by destroying systems of oppression rather than maintaining them, we need not worry about who is ahead, behind, above, or below.

If we can imagine a future in which we are all equal, without a better and a lesser being, we are truly free. Justice is when we all are free from the systems of oppression we suffer.

As we act within our own community, to empower all of us with intersecting identities, so too must we start to examine at a higher level the very systems that cause this hierarchy in the first place. This will include all animalization, otherization, exploitation, etc. These things have no place in a truly free black future. Our focus should be on the systems that oppress us— not ourselves becoming masters of this system.

4 HOW TO

By Julia Feliz Brueck and Diana Lee

You've made the connections and are ready to decenter a movement exploited by whiteness for good. What next? It may be daunting to realize all of the ways in which we, as a society, exploit nonhumans: food, entertainment, clothing, testing... So, yes, it *will* take a bit of relearning; but, once you find alternatives to your favorite products and foods, it will all become second-nature. You may even find yourself enjoying your transition, as it's an opportunity to try completely new things and experiment with new experiences, textiles, products, and foods you probably hadn't ever before thought of trying.

Many people think that veganism is restrictive, but the reality is actually the opposite. We're so used to thinking of our options in a way that actually limits what's available for us and hides the types of foods and practices our communities preferred before colonialism.

Transitioning to a Plant-Based Diet and Vegan Living

Have you ever stopped to consider just how many types of plant foods make part of our meals already? As an Afro-Indigenous Puerto Rican, having grown up on an island in the tropics, I grew up eating staples that are already vegan by default: plantains (tostones, amarillos, mofongo...), yuca, avocado, rice (salted and with a little oil), beans (chickpeas, pigeon peas, red and black beans...), mangoes, papaya, passion fruit...The list goes on! We also have spices and herbs that are already typically vegan, so we have multiple flavors readily available to us.

In essence, going plant-based means relearning to cook by taking away the animal products and/or replacing them. Vegans of Color from various communities have created, or are creating, recipes and food resources on the Web, so I can assure you that you will likely find that someone has veganized meals or drinks specific to your own culture and community. Veganizing our food involves swapping animal products for foods like tofu, seitan, tempeh, and other alternative meats, as well as replacing butter with margarine, and swapping cow milk for one of dozens of plant milks on the market (soy milk and almond milk are favorite!). There are even cheese and egg alternatives. However, not all brands are the same, and your preferred alternatives will be specific to your tastes. If you don't like one brand, try another.

Going plant-based also means exploring different naturally-occurring plant foods, while learning to cook the ones with which you are already familiar in new and exciting ways. Many cultural cuisines are either vegan or vegetarian by default, without relying on "fake meats" or "fake dairy." These can serve as inspiration for at-home cooking or as an easier option for dining out or ordering delivery. Then, there are the myriad vegetables, roots and fungi we are used to thinking of as components of side dishes— mushrooms, potatoes, eggplant, and broccoli, just to name a few— that, when seasoned and cooked affectionately, can be used to create amazing entrees.

Nutrition

The most difficult part of transitioning is not finding things to eat – its wading through all of the misinformation on nutrition associated with plant-based eating. As with any new routines and practices, please ensure that you check in with your health professionals before embarking on a new diet and, above all, do not stop taking any medication on which you depend (we will discuss this more later in the chapter).

Here's a short guide on what you need to know about plant nutrition, based on the most current available evidence-based information:

It can be intimidating at first if your mind jumps from

protein to iron, on top of all of the diet-related questions from well-meaning friends and family, to trust that your newly adopted plant-based diet will provide your body with everything it needs. Fear not; there is no need to worry about malnutrition when switching over to a vegan lifestyle. As long as you eat a full and varied diet, you should have no problem getting the vitamins and nutrients essential to human life on a plant-based diet. In fact, people who consume a diet full of animal products, such as the Standard American Diet (SAD) for example, have to be mindful of many of the same nutrients as those who follow a diet free from nonhuman animals and their byproducts.

There are several important nutrients in which those who eat the SAD diet are consistently deficient. These nutrients include fiber, potassium, magnesium, and vitamins A and C (U.S. Department of Health and Human Services and U.S. Department of Agriculture 2015). This is due to low intake of whole grains, fruits, and vegetables, which are all foods that are highly available on a varied plant-based diet. The vegan diet is also naturally cholesterol-free and may offer health benefits for certain diet-related diseases. Major dietetic associations around the world have confirmed this through evidence-based research, and thus support plant-based diets at all stages of life.

One example is the Academy of Nutrition and Dietetics (AND; formerly the American Dietetic Association). The AND states that:

> It is the position of the Academy of Nutrition and

Dietetics that appropriately planned vegetarian, including vegan, diets are healthful, nutritionally adequate and may provide health benefits for the prevention and treatment of certain diseases. These diets are appropriate for all stages of the life cycle, including pregnancy, lactation, infancy, childhood, adolescence, older adulthood and for athletes. (Melina et al. 2016)

Although plant-based nutrition is healthy and safe, as with any diet, there are nutrients, vitamins, and elements that you should be mindful of while transitioning to plant-based eating. Protein, iron, calcium, vitamin B12, vitamin D, and certain fatty acids are important nutrients of which to keep track. Many of these have multiple important functions in the body; for the sake of simplicity, we'll discuss their most significant roles, why they're important, and how to ensure that you are getting enough of each.

Protein

Protein is the nutrient about which we hear most. As a vegan, you can expect to hear the question "So, where do you get your protein?" often, no matter how long you have been vegan. However, there is no reason to worry about protein as long as you are eating a varied diet. Let's dig into this a little deeper.

According to the National Institute of Health, the recommended daily intake of protein is **0.8 g per kg of**

body weight for maintenance. In other words, if you are not actively trying to gain muscle mass, or if you have not been specifically advised by a medical professional to eat extra protein, then this daily amount is what you should eat (Institute of Medicine 2005). If you are athletic and/or trying to build muscle, this number may rise up to 1.0 or 1.2 g per kg body weight, depending on your goals. If you are pregnant or lactating, these numbers will increase, as well (please consult your doctor and/or registered dietician on your specific nutritional requirements).

Here's how to calculate protein requirements for maintenance purposes for yourself:

> 1. Convert your weight to kilograms by dividing your weight in pounds by 2.2 (if you already measure your weight in kilograms you can skip this step). For example, if you weigh 150 pounds:
>
> **150 pounds ÷ 2.2 pounds/kilogram**
> **= 68 kilograms**
>
> 2. Take your weight in kilograms and multiply it by 0.8 to find out how much protein you need to eat in a day for maintenance.
>
> **68 kilograms x 0.8 grams protein/kilogram**
> **body weight = 55 grams protein**

Therefore, a 150-pound adult needs to eat 55 grams of protein in a day for maintenance. Here is a chart with some weights for quick reference (calculations are rounded to the nearest whole number for simplicity):

Weight (pounds)	Weight (kilograms)	Daily protein requirement (grams)
100	45	36
125	57	45
150	68	55
175	80	64
200	91	73
225	102	82
250	114	91
275	125	100
300	136	109

The topic of protein gets a little bit more complicated when you take **amino acids** into consideration. Amino acids are a family of molecules that come together to make up protein. Your body actually breaks down proteins into their amino acid building blocks, and then recombines them to build its own proteins. There are twenty amino acids that your body uses: eleven of which your body is able to produce on its own, and **nine essential amino acids** that you need to get through what you eat (MedlinePlus 2018). When you hear people talking about **complete protein**, what they mean is that it supplies all nine of these essential amino acids. Soy products are an example of a complete protein (Michelfelder 2009), but, unlike soy, most plant proteins are not complete proteins. A persistent myth is that vegans must carefully match the foods they eat in a single meal in order to get the right protein combinations; however, this was found to be untrue. Young and Pellett (1994) explained that, "Research indicates that an assortment of plant foods eaten over the course of a day can provide all essential amino acids and ensure adequate nitrogen retention and use in healthy adults; thus, complementary proteins do not need to be consumed at the same meal." In essence, in order to meet the nutritional requirements of all nine amino acids, vegans need to simply eat a varied diet throughout the day— just like everyone else.

Reassuringly, the Academy of Nutrition and Dietetics (2016) has found that **the majority of vegans DO meet their protein needs** and may even exceed them. Even the American Heart Association states that it is unnecessary to eat animal products to get enough protein: "Plant proteins alone can provide enough of the essential and non-essential amino acids, as long as sources of dietary protein are varied and caloric intake is high enough to meet energy needs." They explained that, "Whole grains, legumes, vegetables, seeds and nuts all contain both essential and non-essential amino acids. You don't need to consciously combine these foods ("complementary proteins") within a given meal."

Great protein sources for vegans:

- Whole grains
- Legumes (beans)
- Vegetables
- Nuts and seeds
- Vegan meats (tofu, tempeh, seitan, TVP, etc.).

As long as you are eating varied foods throughout the day and you are meeting your caloric needs, you should have no issue meeting your protein needs.

Vegan Bodybuilders and Athletes

Many bodybuilders and athletes find success with a vegan lifestyle. There is a sizeable, and growing, portion of the bodybuilder and athletic communities who have revolutionized their lifestyle by transitioning to fully plant-based diets.

If this is your goal, you will need to consume more protein than maintenance levels. There are many resources available to calculate *macronutrient* (protein, fat, and carbohydrate) targets that take being vegan into consideration.

Soy Products

As previously mentioned, soy products can be a great resource for vegans because soy is a complete protein that is easily digested. There is controversy around soy, however, because of the presence of isoflavones. Isoflavones are classified as phytoestrogens, which means they are plant compounds that look physically similar to the human hormone estrogen. Even though countless studies have demonstrated healthful benefits of consuming soy products, the presence of these phytoestrogens lead to concerns that soy products may have some unwanted effects in humans. Research of the health effects in humans has supported the safety and health of consuming soy products, so much so that the European Food Safety Authority has concluded that soy does not have adverse effects in humans (Messina 2016). Unless you have an allergy, enjoy your soy!

Iron

Iron is an essential nutrient to the human body. Among other things, it is responsible for carrying oxygen all over your body to help your cells make energy. There are two kinds of dietary iron: *heme* and *nonheme* (Abbaspour et al. 2014). Heme iron is found in blood and, therefore, comes from consuming animal meat. Non-heme iron comes from plant sources. Heme iron is more *bioavailable* than nonheme iron, meaning that our bodies are able to digest a higher amount of iron from meat sources than from plant sources. Because of this, the AND recommends that vegans eat 1.8 times the amount of iron that non-vegans eat (Melina et al. 2016). It is also important to keep in mind that menstruating people need to consume more iron than others. The NIH recommends 14 mg of iron daily for non-menstruating vegan adults and 32 mg a day for menstruating vegan adults (National Institute of Health 2018). That being said, iron-deficiency anemia rates in vegans are not any higher than in non-vegans, so there is no need to stress about iron levels. Again, just make sure you are eating plenty of iron-rich plant foods.

Here is a list of vegan foods that are great sources of iron (The Vegan RD 2018):

- Beans
- Soy Foods
- Nuts and seeds
- Vegetables such as winter squashes and dark, leafy greens
- Dried fruits
- Grains such as whole wheat bread, oatmeal, quinoa, and pearl barley

Combining iron with vitamin C increases the bioavailability of the iron in plant foods. Vitamin C is usually pretty abundant in a vegan diet, specifically found in citrus fruits, strawberries, broccoli, tomatoes, and more.

Calcium

Calcium is an important mineral for the body that has many functions, including strengthening the bones and teeth, as well as helping deliver nerve signals that make your muscles move (National Institute of Health 2016).

Adults should aim to eat 1,000 mg of calcium a day. While dairy is usually the first thing most people associate with calcium, there are plenty of ways to get calcium from plants that don't require the cruel practices of dairy farming. According to The Vegan RD, vegans should eat two cups of calcium-rich foods per day (three cups a day if you are over 50).

Calcium-rich foods (The Vegan RD 2018):

- Cooked low-oxalate greens (Chinese cabbage, collard greens, broccoli, mustard greens, or turnip greens)
- Calcium-set tofu
- Fortified plant milks
- Fortified juices

Including these foods in your diet will help you attain your daily requirement for dietary calcium.

Vitamin D

Vitamin D also has many important functions in the body but is most known for helping our bodies absorb calcium. Because of this, it is important in the function of calcium when it comes to building strong bones. Unfortunately, low levels of Vitamin D are extremely common worldwide, affecting almost 50% of the global population (Nair and Maseeh 2012).

There are two ways to get vitamin D (Institute of

Medicine 2011):

1. **Eating foods rich in vitamin D.** There are not many foods that are naturally sufficient sources of vitamin D. This is part of the reason so many people are deficient, most of whom are omnivores.

2. **Sun exposure**; however, many factors can limit the efficiency of this process.

   - More melanin in the skin means better natural protection from UV rays, and better protection from UV rays can decrease your skin's ability to produce Vitamin D. This means that **the darker your skin, the less able you may be to produce enough Vitamin D from sunlight alone.**

   - **Living far from the equator** decreases the amount of direct sunlight to which you are exposed.

   - **The season**. In many climates, you cannot get enough sunlight in fall and winter, but spring and summer is better for sun exposure.

   - **Consistently wearing full-coverage clothing** for religious or personal reasons.

   - **Wearing sunscreen.**

   Because of these limiting factors, it is highly recommended that you eat foods fortified with vitamin D and/or take a vitamin D supplement. Foods that tend to be fortified are plant-based milks, breakfast cereals, and juices. Depending on where you live, it may only be necessary to supplement in the fall and winter but check with your doctor if you have concerns (Vegan Society 2018).

If you do choose to take supplements, be aware that there are two kinds of vitamin D supplements: D2 and D3. D2 is always vegan, but some studies suggest that it is not as effective as D3 to raise the levels of Vitamin D in the blood (Melina et al. 2016). D3 is typically **not** vegan; it is commonly derived from sheep lanolin. However, it can also be made from lichens, in which case it is vegan. There are many vegan D3 supplements available on the market; just make sure the label explicitly states that it is vegan.

Vitamin B-12

So far, all the nutrients discussed are easily attained through plant foods and do not require supplementation to meet adequate levels (although fortified foods are wonderful sources of many nutrients). Vitamin B12 is different. Vitamin B12 works to maintain healthful nerve function, make DNA, and prevent anemia (National Institute of Health 2011). Therefore, a Vitamin B12 deficiency could result in anemia or could turn into irreversible nerve damage. Importantly, B12 is produced by bacteria that live either in soil or in intestines. Some animals are able to absorb the B12 they produce in their own intestines, but humans cannot. Even so, many farmed animals are provided with supplementation to ensure they have adequate B12 levels.

It is a common myth that certain plant foods, such as algae or tempeh, contain B12. Currently, no plant foods have been shown to be able to effectively raise vitamin B12 levels in humans. The good news is that we can access the B12 that we need and can absorb directly from the bacteria that produce it (Vegan Society 2018). Therefore, going straight to the source, vegans get the B12 that they need from foods fortified with vitamin B12 and supplements. It's possible to take a supplement every day that gives you between 25 and 100 mcg of vitamin B12 or a supplement once a week that gives you 1,000 mcg (The Vegan RD 2018).

Fatty Acids

There are three main omega-3 fatty acids which are important for optimal health and brain function. Those fatty acids are ALA (alpha-linolenic acid), DHA (docosahexaenoic acid), and EPA (eicosapentaenoic acid). ALA is easy for vegans to get enough of by eating foods like flaxseeds, hemp seeds, walnuts, and some oils. However, since vegans don't eat seafood or eggs, they can have low amounts of the fatty acids DHA and EPA (Melina et al. 2016).

DHA and EPA can be synthesized from ALA, so it is not considered necessary to have a dietary source (The Vegan RD 2018); however, there may be healthful benefits to supplementing these fatty acids. You can easily get vegan DHA and EPA supplements that are made out of algae, and not from fish or eggs.

Variety Goes a Long Way

Even though some people in mainstream culture fear that vegans don't get adequate nutrition, this is a myth. Dietary organizations across the world have released papers in support of plant-based diets at all stages of life. It's important to eat a varied diet rich in all types of plant foods, supplement your diet with vitamins B12 and D3, and eat fortified foods as needed. In this way, you will get all the nutrients your body needs to thrive, and you can reap the rewards that many find in a vegan lifestyle.

If health is a dietary motive for you, it is important to keep in mind that "vegan" doesn't inherently equate with "healthy." Even though the vegan diet has zero cholesterol and tends to be lower in fat and higher in fiber and other vitamins than an omnivorous diet, there are still food choices that can be harmful to your health. Foods that are heavily processed, or foods that are high in fats and sugars are full of "empty" calories, which means that they are high in calories but low in nutritional content. To avoid this, try to fill your diet with plenty of whole foods: foods that are close to how they grow in plant form and are minimally processed, such as vegetables and whole grains.

While whole-food veganism is not a cure-all, vegans

do often enjoy many health benefits, including lower cholesterol, lower risk of heart disease, lower blood pressure, lower risk of type II diabetes, and lower rates of cancer (Melina et al. 2016).You can feel safe in knowing that while choosing a vegan lifestyle takes further steps against cruelty and oppression of both non-human animals and humans, your body may also benefit in several ways.

Beyond Food

Veganism isn't just about what we eat. It's about taking a firm, active, and consistent stance against human supremacy and, ultimately, disrupting the ability that we give white supremacy to use animalization and speciesism as a tool against us– also in conjunction with capitalism and other systems of oppression working together against true liberation. Because of this, we must also reject all forms of exploitation related to nonhumans that go beyond our diets.

The ways in which nonhumans are oppressed are numerous and seem never ending. Apart from food and diet, their oppression is tied to main forms of exploitation that include their commodification and exploitation for testing, entertainment, clothing, and even as "pets."

There are a vast number of websites, books, and other resources that break down the horrific ways in which society otherizes nonhumans in order to render them commodities. and how their lives are ended after their short, abused lives. At this point, even if you don't particularly like a person, we can agree that abuse and oppression of any form towards any being is not justifiable, especially when we have another choice. We do hope that you will make a commitment to let yourself truly see the many different ways that nonhumans are exploited once you are ready to face just how deep the oppression and system goes. It usually begins with nonhumans, but when you look deeper, you will see just how their suffering is tied to ours.

Within these systems, however, there are instances, as in the case of medication and vaccines, where vegan alternatives may not exist. Thus, this becomes part of a root issue that needs to be addressed outside individual control. Veganism is not about perfectionism; it is about doing as much as we can in a collective effort to take down systems of oppression that work side by side to prevent us from real change. It is about making the choice that is least exploitative when you can make it and supporting efforts working on root issues rather than targeting individuals with dependency on some of these systems. For example, even though medication and vaccines may be tested on animals, it is important that we recognize that those who are dependent on medications for their physical and mental health must continue to take their medications and that, instead of demonizing them for doing so, we must advocate for anti-oppressive alternatives from the appropriate industries. Those of us with the appropriate background knowledge may also seek to create these alternatives ourselves.

What about other forms of exploitation?

Animal testing: One area in which we do have vegan options are in the products that we use. Cleaning products, washing detergents, toiletries, and even make-up are examples of products in which non-animal-tested alternatives readily exist.

Entertainment: Nonhuman animal forms of exploitation that are tied to entertainment include circuses, zoos, fishing, horse and dog racing, hunting, aquariums, and more. Alternatives include gymnastics-based circuses (such as Cirque du Soleil); nature centers, as well as state and national parks, which often offer nature programs to get to know your local wildlife; snorkeling; and wildlife documentaries, in which you can see what these animals are like in their own homes instead of in unnatural, confined spaces. Arguments for some of these spaces, like zoos and aquariums, often revolve around conservation efforts; however, without addressing root issues— in this case, the actual reason why these nonhumans are threatened in nature— it makes it even that much more senseless to confine them in the name of "conservation." While this list of alternatives is not extensive, we encourage you to look further into finding alternatives that work specifically for you.

Clothing: Leather and fur are not very different from one another. One is the flesh of a nonhuman, while the other is the flesh with the hair still attached to it. Other forms of animal skin, hair, and bodies used for clothing include wool and silk. There are synthetic and plant-based alternatives, which make these intensely cruel industries obsolete. Not only are there myriad textiles that are already vegan, like cotton, but also there are alternatives that look like leather and fur, so that you don't even have to alter your signature style or fashion preferences in order to switch to vegan clothing. Faux-leather and faux-fur are not only more ethical than their animal-based alternatives, but they are also much, *much* more affordable!

Pets: Breeders continue to add to the millions of dogs, cats, rabbits, and other nonhumans exploited as "pets" who die in pounds each year. Others— like birds, reptiles, and even fish— are stolen from their natural habitats, leaving the wild populations in peril, to be sold in shops and kept in cages. "Released"/abandoned or escaped "pets" may add to the invasive species problem, in which nonnative species overtake and destroy natural habitats and native species. Once established, non-native invasive species, including plants, are very difficult to stop as they overtake native areas. Alternatives that work against a system that commodifies nonhumans for human pleasure include adoption, fostering, rescuing, and volunteering with organizations working to ensure nonhumans do not continue to die senselessly. When adopting a nonhuman animal, it is also important to make a commitment to take care of them for the duration of their lives. They are not merely "pets" but companion animals that become a part of our families as the individuals they are, rather than the anonymous members of a mass group as which we often see them.

Animal Agriculture: Some of the many topics you should study further in order to get a complete picture of why eating animals is harmful, beyond its impact on your own body, include:

Environmental racism: Indigenous land rights abuse, climate change in regions populated by People of Color, deforestation in the Global South, pollution.

Human Abuses: The plight of farm laborers and slaughterhouse workers worldwide, exploitation of migrants.

Nonhuman Animal Abuses: Slaughtering practices, castration, debeaking, forced insemination, tail docking, mulesing, cruel live transport, intensive confinement, loss of natural wildlife habitats and decimation of biodiversity.

Nonhumans are rarely afforded rights from abuses tied to the animal agriculture industry, which usually take their lives before adulthood. For instance, animal cruelty laws in the U.S. do not apply to common animal agriculture practices such as debeaking, forced insemination, and castration. Meanwhile, any of these same acts committed against a dog or a cat would qualify the offending human to be brought up on animal cruelty charges. While the ethical implications of slaughter as the end are clear, there are industry practices that are cruel yet standard and tied to most of these industries, including within dairy and egg production. Labels like "humane," "organic," and "free-range" tend to mean very little to nothing in the case of how nonhumans are actually treated (Rodríguez 2018).

***

The above guide is but a starting point towards learning more about the ways in which nonhumans are devalued within our society. It is imperative that you continue to research the how, their effects on our own communities, and even the similarities in justification for their exploitation even though our oppressions are vastly very different to theirs.

Cited Works

Abbaspour, N., Hurrell, R., and Kelishadi, R. (2014). Review on iron and its importance for human health. *J Res Med Sci.*19(2): 164-174.

Institute of Medicine (2011) Committee to Review Dietary Reference Intakes for Vitamin D and Calcium; Ross A.C., Taylor C.L., Yaktine A.L., et al., editors. *Dietary Reference Intakes for Calcium and Vitamin D.* National Academies Press, U.S.

Institute of Medicine (2005). Dietary Reference Intakes for Energy, Carbohydrate, Fiber, Fat, Fatty Acids, Cholesterol, Protein, and Amino Acids. *The National Academies Press.*

MedlinePlus: Medical Encyclopedia (2018) *Amino Acids.* US National Library of Medicine. Accessed May 26, 2018: https://medlineplus.gov

Melina, V., Craig, W., and Levin, S. (2016). Position of the American Dietetic Association: Vegetarian Diets. *J Acad Nutr Diet*. 116(12).

Messina, M. (2016). Soy and Health Update: Evaluation of the Clinical and Epidemiologic Literature. *Nutrients*. 8(12): 754.

Michelfelder, A.J. (2009). Soy: a complete source of protein. *Am Fam Physician*. 1; 79(1):43-7.

Nair, R. and Maseeh, A. (2012). Vitamin D: The "sunshine" vitamin. *J Pharmacol Pharmacother*. 3(2): 118-126.

National Institute of Health (2016). Calcium Fact Sheet for Consumers. *NIH.gov*: Accessed May 26, 2018: https://ods.od.nih.gov/factsheets/Calcium-Consumer/

National Institute of Health (2018). Iron Fact Sheet for Health Professionals. *NIH.gov*. Accessed May 26, 2018: https://ods.od.nih.gov/factsheets/Iron-HealthProfessional/

National Institute of Health (2011). Vitamin B12 Fact Sheet for Consumers. *NIH.gov*: https://ods.od.nih.gov/factsheets/VitaminB12-Consumer/

Rodríguez, S. (2018). Food Justice: A Primer. *Sanctuary Publishers*.

The American Heart Association (2018). Vegetarian

Diets. *Heart.org*. Accessed October 12, 2018:
http://www.heart.org/HEARTORG/HealthyLiving/Healthy
Eating/VegetarianDiets_UCM_306032_Article.jsp

The Vegan RD (2018). Calcium: A Vegan Nutrition Primer.
Theveganrd.com. Accessed May 26, 2018 May 26:
https://www.theveganrd.com/vegan-nutrition-
101/vegan-nutrition-primers/calcium-a-vegan-nutrition-
primer/

The Vegan RD (2018). Iron: A Vegan Nutrition Primer.
Theveganrd.com. Accessed October 12, 2018:
http://www.theveganrd.com/vegan-nutrition-
101/vegan-nutrition-primers/iron-a-vegan-nutrition-
primer/

The Vegan RD (2018). Vitamin B12: A Vegan Nutrition
Primer. *Theveganrd.com*. Accessed October 12, 2018:
http://www.theveganrd.com/vegan-nutrition-
101/vegan-nutrition-primers/vitamin-b12-a-vegan-
nutrition-primer/

The Vegan RD (2018). Omega-3 Fats in Vegan Diets: A
Quick Primer. *Theveganrd.com*. Accessed October 12,
2018: https://www.theveganrd.com/2012/01/omega-3-
fats-in-vegan-diets-a-quick-primer/

U.S. Department of Health and Human Services and U.S.
Department of Agriculture (2015). *Dietary Guidelines for
Americans – 2015-2020*. 8th Edition.

Vegan Society (2018). What Every Vegan Should Know
About Vitamin B12. *The Vegan Society*. Accessed May 26,

2018: https://www.vegansociety.com/resources/
nutrition-and-health/nutrients/vitamin-b12/what-every-
vegan-should-know-about-vitamin-b12

Vegan Society (2018) Why do we need vitamin D in our
diets? *The Vegan Society*. Accessed May 26, 2018:
https://www.vegansociety.com/resources/nutrition-and-
health/nutrients/vitamin-d

Young, V.R. and Pellett, P.L. (1994). Plant proteins in
relation to human protein and amino acid nutrition. *Am J
Clin Nutr.* 59(suppl): 1203S-1212S.

5 A FINAL NOTE

A Stance against White Supremacy Itself
By Julia Feliz Brueck and Destiny "Desy" Whitaker

In 2018, the U.S. Census Bureau projected that white people will become the minority within the U.S. in about twenty years; however, despite becoming the majority, People of Color will still continue to be affected by actions, policies, and systems of oppression invoked by them unless we collectively and consistently work against these. To do this and truly liberate ourselves from white supremacy and colonialism will involve examining the ways in which our own communities have been taught to imitate what was done to us and how we mimic oppressive practices over other marginalized communities, such as nonhuman animals, those most affected by anti-Blackness and anti-Indigeneity, neuro-divergent people, those with disabilities, members of the LGBTQPIA+ community, especially Black Trans Women, those whose income is less than our own, etc.

Furthermore, when we talk about climate change and what we must do RIGHT NOW to abate its effects, which the United Nations (Carus 2010) and many others have asserted includes the wide adoption of plant-based diets, we must be clear that this is not a reflection of whiteness. Taking action is imperative in order to work towards creating a world that will be better and safer for our own. It's time that we detach our responsibility to protect our planet and our most marginalized from whiteness itself. People of Color will be (and already are) the ones who suffer most from the effects of climate change, and we cannot afford to be tools of white supremacy or uphold the tools it uses to keep us oppressed. We all know People of Color have been and are the most affected by systems of oppression that we have been tricked into supporting ourselves: capitalism, the destruction of our planet and other living beings, supremacy over other humans and nonhumans, and the list goes on. It's a never-ending cycle of supremacist views and ideology that we follow without realizing they keep us oppressed and in the background. Decenter whiteness and why we need to act when we can and how we can will suddenly make sense.

This book emerged from the need to decenter the idea that Vegans of Color are upholding whiteness, coupled with a desire to engage in the collective effort to end white supremacy once and for all. Many of us have internalized the idea that our voices will never be heard above whiteness. Despite this, we still try. We speak with no script or guideline and may even fumble as we attempt to explain some of the interconnections that have led us to make this decision – a decision that makes sense as the best in our fight against systemic oppression for ourselves and others. While veganism is not a cure-all (both figuratively and literally) nor an immediate fix, rejecting all systems of supremacy, including our own power over nonhuman animals, is to take an active stance against white supremacy itself.

As you turn the last page, remember that there are already People of Color, including Black and Indigenous People of Color (BIPoC), who readily embrace veganism as an active commitment to *consistent anti-oppression*. There are disabled vegans. There are poor vegans. There are poor, disabled PoC, and there are PoC whose identities intersect in more than one way. Vegans of Color are not the products of one-dimensional whiteness that readily shames us, tone polices us, and screams in our faces while ignoring how it forced this system upon us in the first place. Deanna Jacobsen Koepke (2007) explained that, *In the United States, our society is stratified and structured along race, class, and gender lines, such that some lives are considered more valuable than others*. Colonialism introduced and implemented a capitalist system (McCraw 1999) in which those considered "less than" continue to be justifiably exploited for gains. This very system, according to Jacobsen Koepke, thrives on "isms" in order to otherize communities and keep the power within the hands of the most privileged. Capitalism made nonhumans part of that equation with their introduction for purposeful exploittation and their use by colonizers as tools of extermination (Brosnan and Blackwell 2016) and otherization under white supremacy against marginalized humans. Thus, it is vital that we recognize that in order to take power away from intersecting oppressions linked to one another forged under white supremacy, we must include a stance against human supremacy in our consistent fight against all "isms". Only through this consistency will it be possible to collapse systems of oppression effectively as a whole.

In essence, *Veganism of Color* – like all other social justice movements aimed at creating a safer, more healthful, and more just world— does not belong to any one community. It is an instrument available to us to ensure that the pursuit of justice for humans and nonhumans is propelled forward while consistently challenging, rather than replicating, any form of supremacy.

Cited Works

Brosnan, K. and Blackwell, J. (2016). Agriculture, Food, and the Environment. *Oxford Research Encyclopedia of American History.* Ed.

Carus, F. (2010). UN Urges Global Move to Meat and Dairy Free Diet. *The Guardian.*

Koepke, D. (2007). Race, Class, Poverty, and Capitalism. *Race, Gender & Class, 14*(3/4), 189-205.

McCraw, T. (1999). It Came in the First Ships: Capitalism in America. *Harvard Business School*:

https://hbswk.hbs.edu/item/it-came-in-the-first-ships-capitalism-in-america

U.S. Census Bureau (2018). *Older People Projected to Outnumber Children for First Time in U.S. History*. U.S. Census Bureau Newsroom. Accessed January 12, 2018.

6 ABOUT THE CONTRIBUTORS

Editor

Julia Feliz Brueck, M.Sc. is a published author, editor, and illustrator with a background in science and the arts. Julia is also the founder of Sanctuary Publishers, a book publisher that works to give back to marginalized communities. Her work includes building bridges between social justice movements and consistent anti-oppression activism. Julia's previous published book titles include the *Baby and Toddler Vegan Feeding Guide* and *Veganism in an Oppressive World: A Vegans-of-Color Community Project.* The children's book *Wild and Free,* by Andrea Zimmer, features her colorful illustrations.

Writers

Doreen Akiyo Yomoah is a Ghanaian writer working in Geneva, Switzerland. Her writing focuses mainly on social justice and human rights issues.

Nekeisha Alayna Alexis is an independent scholar and activist with wide-ranging interests in race/racism, human and nonhuman oppression, intersectionality, and co-liberation with other animals. She also studies Christian ethics and theology concerning nonhuman animals. In addition to her academic work, Nekeisha is involved in local organizing around other animals and other social justice concerns.

Linda Alvarez, Ph.D. has been involved in animal rights advocacy and activism for twenty years and is dedicated to spreading awareness on animal liberation and issues of food (in)justice in Communities of Color. Linda holds a Ph.D. in Political Science and a Master of International Relations from Claremont Graduate University. She also holds a Master of Latin American Studies from California State University, Los Angeles. Her scholarly interests revolve around exploring the ways in which underrepresented and marginalized groups interact, challenge and resist dominant structures of power. As a political scientist, she works within the frameworks of comparative political behavior, political psychology, transnational migration, social movements, race and ethnic politics, food politics, and the study of violence and trauma among underrepresented and marginalized populations.

Kamekə Brown developed a passion for exploring the power of multi-species community and the practices we can engage in to achieve collective healing and liberation through a decade of work with nonprofits and farmed animal sanctuaries. She resides in California with her canine partners, Chaz and Kaia.

Shahada Chowdhury is part of the Bangladeshi diaspora living in the U.K. Shahada is currently working towards their B.Sc. in Psychology and organizes with a Marxist group that works to educate locals about social justice and class issues.

Towani Duchscher, Ph.D. dances in the liminal space between her roles and identities of dancer, poet, mother, wife, Black, white, woman, teacher, and vegan. She holds a PhD in Educational Research in Curriculum and Learning from the University of Calgary, in Calgary, Alberta, Canada. Her research examines the somatic lessons of the hidden curriculum through arts-based research. She reconsiders the choices made in schools and seeks hierarchy-attenuating approaches to teaching social justice for all beings.

Cina Ebrahimi is from Seattle, Washington, and has been involved in the struggle for the rights of humans and other animals since 2004.

Carolyn Ienna is a writer and performer working under the MC name Rap Attack. She is a Wiradjuri/Sicilian woman working to educate people through her creative art about injustice in order to combat it. Carolyn has been vegan since around 1985.

Jael Israel is a London-based complementary therapist, nutritional therapist-in-training, teacher, and vegan chef. Her activist interests include food accessibility, heritage and legacy, and healthcare advocacy.

Rama Ganesan was born in Chennai, India. At the age of ten, she emigrated to the UK with her parents. As an adult, she then emigrated to the United States with her spouse. Rama now lives in Indiana and has two grown children, two cat companions, and one dog companion.

Prateek Gautam is from Basti, UP, India. He is an IT graduate and a Dalit, ambedkarite, and vegan activist. Prateek is also a musician, focusing on the guitar while also producing and mixing various forms of music.

Diana Lee has been vegan since 2017 and currently works as a digital marketer specialist for an animal rescue nonprofit. Her background is in food science and biochemistry, with research focused on the potential of antioxidants in plant foods to reverse disease and improve health.

Namita Money is an artist, activist, and community organizer in the DC area who strives to adopt compassion and mindfulness into all of their work. Their deep connection to nonhuman animals inspires them to advocate for humans to live more compassionately and less wastefully, and to raise and support the voices of all marginalized communities— no matter the species.

Danielle Moore is a vegan living at the intersections of black queer fat neurodivergent womanhood. She currently lives on the lands of the Gadigal people of the Eora nation ("Sydney, Australia" to the British) and spends her efforts on decolonizing education for her child, as well as writing under "The Black Queer Vegan Diaries." Dani holds a Bachelor of Management Information Systems, as well as a Master of Business Administration and has fifteen years' experience in software engineering and lean engineering consulting.

Jocelyn Ramirez is a young, disabled, Mexican-American high fem, born and raised in the Humboldt Park and Logan Square hoods of Chicago. While her work primarily centers reproductive justice for youth, she is also passionate about achieving health/healing, queer, disability, food, and racial justice in her communities.

Saryta Rodríguez is an author, editor, and social justice advocate. Their past writings have focused on food justice, veganism, race, and gentrification. Saryta is the author of the books *Food Justice: A Primer* (2018) and

Until Every Animal is Free (2015). They also contributed an essay ("Move to Berkeley! and Other Follies") and part of the Introduction to *Veganism in an Oppressive World: A Vegans-of-Color Community Project* (2017). Saryta also specializes in literacy tutoring for student in Grades K-12, and edits manuscripts of all genres for independent authors and publishing houses.

Kez St. Louis is a gender-expansive trans man of Afro-Caribbean descent. He is currently a student at Ramapo College of New Jersey with a focus on Integrated Science and a minor in Food Studies. Kez currently works at the Ali Forney Center, an organization for homeless LGBTQIA+ youth.

Destiny "Desy" Whitaker is a Black 17-year-old who is also neurodivergent, chronically ill, and a member of the LGBTQIA+ community. She loves the arts and volunteering. Destiny strives to ensure that all oppressed communities (especially those with intersectional identities) are represented in the projects in which she partakes.

Ayoola M. White came to veganism through a lifelong interest in environmentalism. As a practitioner of library science, she is interested in the connections between information literacy, food justice, and social justice.

Graphic Designer

Danae Silva Montiel is a professional illustrator and graphic designer based in Mexico. Danae has been vegan for half her life and enjoys living an existence that leads her to experience the uniqueness of living in different places.

Cover Artist

Meneka Repka, Ph.D. is an artist and teacher living in Calgary, Alberta. She earned a Ph.D. in education in 2017 and is interested in arts-based research, eco and environmental pedagogies, and consistent anti-oppression.

Grant Support

Deutscher Jugendschutz-Verband is a German-registered non-profit organization that aims to improve the lives of future generations by supporting a wide variety of projects, especially led by marginalized groups or individuals doing work within the social justice spectrum.

Made in the USA
Monee, IL
22 December 2019